SONGS FOR

SONGS FOR THE UNSUNG

Edited by Joy Howard

GREY HEN

First published in 2017 by Grey Hen Press
PO Box 269
Kendal
Cumbria
LA9 9FE
www.greyhenpress.com

ISBN   978-0-9933756-4-4
Collection Copyright © Joy Howard 2017

Printed by Flexpress, Birstall, Leicester LE4 3BY

For all of us

Our lives begin to end the day we become silent about things that matter.

Martin Luther King

Preface

Some years ago I ran a workshop with the title of this book as its subject matter. I was expecting, and got, several moving poems about the obscure lives of friends and relatives, poems which illuminated the sometimes unappreciated impact of those closest to us. Since then the idea of an anthology on the theme has been brewing. The original idea of a book celebrating the familiar broadened; I realised that the scope could be far larger. When the time felt right, I came back to this idea with a different perspective encompassing the marginalised, the alienated, the suffering, the frequently ignored or despised but courageous individuals who people our world and sent out a call for poems on forgotten lives with as wide a brief as possible. I was amazed by the scope and depths of the response. I have been deeply moved, and learned much.

It is the contributing poets who have shaped this book. The world feels like a better place for their ability to enter, and shine a light on, the lives of others. These poems help us recognise that we are all world citizens, however or wherever we are situated, and whatever our own good or bad fortune in the present time.

Joy Howard

Contents

a path to nowhere

all those back-breaking months

between the lines

postlude

Prelude

Other

You banished me under the sun and moon
and under the stars you stripped me bare.
You made me stand while everyone stared.
You gave me away as nought.

I wade through fields towards the sea
searching for somewhere safe to stay.
But hedgerows rise and the mist betrays.
Will anyone hear my voice?

Susanna Harding

a moth on your cheek

Tonight I Met Someone

Just someone with a sad edge
who sat beside me, tic of a smile,
chose me for some inapt reason
to share a few words though
they seemed hard-found.

Minutes, fifteen maybe, at the most,
and in that time (was it taken from
or added to his own?) told me
how his life is now.

Occasional, lonely, the choices he makes,
his small achievements and desires.
Why me? Innocuous, perhaps, more likely
than synergy. I absorbed it all,
nodded here, smiled there.

Nothing changed. No one was saved,
no great deed was done. Nothing was found
or lost, nothing given in this bare exchange,
not a name, not even a shake of hands.

And I was glad of him, his choosing me,
our sharing minutes with no outcome,
no duty to connect. I need reminding,
sometimes, of the simple things.
Humanity. A reason to exist.

Anne Stewart

Territories

Encapsulated behind plate glass
the earnest pleasure-seekers go about
replenishing their transitory certainties.
A glass of Bourgogne Aligote to wash down
thin slices of pan-fried foie gras
on toasted brioche with salad
of bitter leaves.

Beyond the window an old woman
angles across the street, like someone
bending before winds that flatten
the Hungarian plain. Certain
of her territory among the dispossessed,
she clasps a carrier bag swollen
with bitter memories.

Elisabeth Rowe

Washed-up Woman

Afterwards, nobody could remember asking her.
Yet there she was, up to here in suds,
saying *someone's got to do it* and
it won't take a moment

Afterwards, we remembered how
she sat at the table's end, next to the difficult child.
The out of practice small talk,
the old fashioned clothes. We guessed
she was someone's second cousin,
someone's aunt.

But when it was she left her chair
and was later found at the sink
waving away the family with a yellow-gloved hand,
no-one could remember.

Who was it said the unkind thing
that sent her scampering home?

Ann Alexander

Reconstructing a Brother

It's not easy to piece him together
to fill in the gaps
with my own stories
or stories you and you and you
have made up.

I can see patches, stitches
holes filled with shadow
where the stuffing
has been ripped out

vein pulsing on his forehead
beard grey, untrimmed.

I put words in his mouth
those I think I remember
those he committed to tape.
They spurt out, slur
onto the carpet.

I dress him in a rugby shirt
can't remember
did he wear jeans?

At times he is in
two places at once
where he said he was
and where he said he was.

The props are easy
fencing mask, pint of beer
succession of long-dead dogs
jostling his heels.

Even as I work
pick up a piece
I've rummaged out –
a photograph perhaps
try to make it fit –
another is dropping off

He won't look me in the eyes.
I can't remember
if he ever did.

Jennie Osborne

After Tim

I haven't thought of him for years: the baby
we might have accepted but didn't.
I'd thought I'd like to call him Tim.

I saw a man with his name to day and remembered.
He'll be in his thirties too, like Will
who would have become his older brother.

Someone will have embraced him who felt more confident
that they could meet with wisdom whatever came
of the question-mark he carried in his genes.

After we let him go we adopted Liz
and when she was nearly two we moved away.
If it hadn't been for the wobble we'd had over Tim

Liz and Jay would have lived in orbits that never touched
and they would never have created Isla. Or Teddy.
Which, if you've met them, is inconceivable.

Frances Nagle

Woman Through Binoculars

I watch you scutter in and out,
upping roots like some strange pet
and nose around your loneliness.

Rain needles in and ghosts my sight.
I carry you in my cupped hands
under a flat and blackened sky.

Smudged and still against a door
you watch the boat; its pitch and cut
slips silver fish towards the gulls.

You choose to scream: I cannot hear
but only see your head thrown back
mouth wide, but nothing coming out.

Hilary Stobbs

From Torbay to Newton Abbott

All eyes measure him. I draw the short straw.
He throttles the pole beside my seat,
his tattoos an aide memoir:
I am a warrior. I was loved once.

He wears the story of his life on neck, on arms –
all the parts you see bear testament.
The hair is Genghis. Shaved, a pony tail on top
to lift him up to God.

Our eyes meet. I am in Sunday Best
but we, roughly the same age,
must tolerate each other on this country ride.

The thick coat smells of sleeping rough,
when coat becomes a pillow for the head,
all clothes worn, for fear of theft or cold.

He asks, politely: is it ok if I sit alongside you?
And then for seven miles
I wear his breath, as he explains
where he's going now, and where he's been.

Ann Alexander

The Patron Saint of America

An African-American woman in red uniform,
an earth-bound air hostess, is stationed
at the hub of the huge hotel, of a milling
mass of 9,000 delegates, calling out all day,
May I help someone?
May I help someone?

And they are drawn to her for guidance
Down the hall.   Up the elevator.
You're welcome.   You're welcome.
All day her voice rises above the rabble.
A voice to lead a gospel choir, of a person
who has found her place in the world.

May I help someone?
May I help someone?
She casts the words about her
like a net of stars and stripes
gathering the shoals of poor,
the lost and huddled masses.

Maggie Butt

Woman in a Fur Coat Reading a Dictionary

From the safety of the store room
behind the issue desk
we, the junior staff, mock her:
'Duchess of the Dictionary's back.'
'Look at that Oxfam chic.'
'It's warm for it today.'
'Bet there's nothing underneath.'
'Bet the book's upside-down
and she can't read. Go look!'

They push me out towards the table
where she sits, fur collar up
against cold winds of scrutiny.
I go right past her, shelve awhile,
then come back and manage
to peep over her shoulder
into the hefty volume.
It's open right way up
at part way through the Cs.

So far as I can tell, she reads.
And wondering if she means
to know all words before she tackles
History or Literature or Law
or if she wants to write
her own story, I try
to think up witty jokes
to take back to my friends
but find somehow I can't.

Like the tutor of a willing
but weak pupil, I want
to shield the mute persistence
of this woman, persuade the world
that what she's doing here
will prove worthwhile. Although
she hasn't finished yet with C,
for me she's moving far
beyond caricature.

Janet Loverseed

It Is Written

On a wall in Ten Bell Lane
JANICE DURRANT IS A HOUR.
Stained red letters seep
as the wind spins
and the sun climbs roofs.
She may be one of the Horae
marking the season in her way
bringing body warmth
rolling clouds apart.
Or a grape-eyed houri,
But this city is no Paradise.
Seems the speller's hand wants
To feel the weight of a punch.
Striking the hour.
For weeks she has not
protested. Hers not come.
Who is she?
And where has she gone?

Jenny Morris

Bird Woman

On a bench by the station
sits a woman feeding birds.

Talk to her, or offer her money
and she'll give you an earful.

Her teeth are gone, knees gape wide
beneath a sacking cape and skirt

as bags spill out a remnant life
across the pavement.

Her face is clenched against the light
but her hands are open, feeding birds.

Angela Kirby

Her Photo

I filch memories from other heads.
For example this photo (source unknown) taken
When summer was dense among the leaves:
Not waking not sleeping, the fine hair flowing back.

The colour of the day still sparkles
In her absence on the tip of my tongue; the words
I can't hear, that were settling round her,
Return at times like the swallows with the songs and names.

M R Peacocke

Crypsis

One winter her old fur coat turns
white as a snowshoe hare, scarves
come arctic out of coloured washes.

If she stands still, walls leak into her:
in the bathroom she's *london clay*
or *windsor white* to match the tiling.

Chair arms grow knuckles when she sits,
the furniture buds legs and feet,
she's cushioned, paneled, carpeted.

She's careful not to lie on grass
in case of mistakes by lawn mowers;
when riled she deepens despite herself.

Wooden fences are comforting
with their spirals and imperfections.
A beech hedge can warm the blood.

Night-walking holds no terrors now.
Ashen moon, black shape in blackness,
a moth on your cheek as she passes.

Kate Rutter

among the dispossessed

The Knock

The sun is rising when the soldiers come.
The snow is pink edged and mauve,
their boot prints deep and blue.
The girl who loves all living things is asleep.

It is summer when the knock comes
and the cherry trees are in full leaf.
The whitewashed farm smells of bread.
There's a woodpecker she thinks,

for the rapping is loud and insistent,
then her father's voice is at the door
and now her mother's here and her brother
and her sister whose hand she must hold

while they pack the sledge with food
and warm clothes and blankets.
The soldiers are waiting in a truck
that puffs dark clouds into the air.

A bird is in the cherry tree. A crow she thinks.
She's wearing her new blazer under her coat.
She has her paints inside her jumper,
some pencils and a notebook.

Her father helps her into the back.
There are canvas flaps she can see out of.
The dog they couldn't take is running after them,
running and running until it can't run anymore.

Pat Winslow

A Miracle at Iskitim

In Siberia, a symbol –
this is what the locals believe,
a magical birth of water:

a fresh water spring, a spurt
close to the ground, a low white
eternal flame.
              We dip our cups
(plastic, from the hotel) and say,
'It tastes pure. The water is pure.'

Some people here heard the last trucks
grind out of sight, after they shut
the 'lagpunkt',
              the slow-killing place,
left the scar for people like us
in a half circle, dark barrels

in our padded coats, gloves, hats, scarves ...
With our white breaths, we breathe out lives
as we raise up transparent cups,

       'The future came too late.'

Dilys Wood

In her *Gulag, A History* (Penguin, 2004) Anne Applebawm refers to a new fresh-water
spring near a former camp at Iskatim.

from **Facts on the Ground**

Today Wales has been spirited away
by fog, like that Mabinogi story
where the king and queen awake
to nothingness – court, courtiers,
fields of barley, sheep, pigs, peasants,
steam from horses, smoke from hearths,
all uncreated as if Genesis
had gone into reverse. Even
the nearest trees look insubstantial

As his olive groves that aren't
there any more must look
to a Palestinian farmer
on the wrong side
of the bored boy with the Uzi.

Stevie Krayer

The Jewish Cemetery in Penzance

The black-clad strangers off the Holland boat
look about them, sniff the fishy air.

The Cornishmen who labour on the quay
squint sideways at the trunks, the bags,
the stone-faced women standing well apart.

What horror made them leave their homes
to wash up here, the first, last town in Britain
(just don't call it England, mind),
battling the weather in 1732?
Trippers, down from England, empty their pockets
and leave. These are other.

One stranger speaks for all. Removes his broad hat.
Begs directions in his courtly English.
No-one understands. The stranger tries again,
doubles up with Dutch. No luck.

A Cornishman stands forth, and speaks.
No-one understands.
Pensans a'gas Dynergh
The harbourmaster comes, interprets.
Penzance welcomes you.
The fishermen turn back
to their slippery trade.

A donkey cart is summoned, and the troupe
clatters up the street to find their small hotel.
This is their rough beginning.

This Jewish cemetery the journey's end,
fifty gravestones, facing east in the wild south west.
Names carved in Hebrew script, in Cornish stone,
tell of silversmiths, distillers of rum, merchants,
loving husbands, wives, who found a refuge here,
prospered, and died.
At rest, at last, behind a Cornish wall.

Ann Alexander

She Pictures her House in a Hundred Years

'He has reduced the population....weeding out the lazy
and dissolute and deporting them to the mainland'
Royal Cornwall Gazette, mid 19th century

Wind has salted, dried and scattered thatch
over the northern rocks. Rain cripples the beams.
My hearth's a garden of buttercup and nettle,
two foxgloves swaying in the chimney corner.

Lichen-covered blocks that refuse to fall
shelter a floor of ragwort and wild agapanthus.
The windowsill where children sat in line, eyes
fixed on the bread oven, chokes with bracken.

Look. A spider has fixed her web to a stalk of grass
stretched tall. Her second guide rope's fastened
to a curling stem of fern and thus she thinks,
if spiders think, that she's secure, embedded.

Kate Rutter

Clearances – South Harris

Scoured by the tide rim   our feet
on the shell sand   a sea folk

of bold winds and wave break   we leaned
into land that was cloak to our back

Now waiting for winter   we sit
in our strangeness   we stare

for a shadow of land makes a bruise
at the sky's edge   but here

should only be light   only red
ebb of sun   over silver and green

We watch through a grey fade
of day   we are gone

where waveless dark water is stirring
the brown knots of wrack

and westward behind us is standing
a wall of rough rock

Joy Howard

During the first half of the 18th century, the crofters from the fertile machair of the
Atlantic seaboard were forcibly removed to the inhospitable east coast to make way
for sheep farming.

Christina MacDonald 1881

I had to come to work and earn my keep
to serve the Quarry Master and his son,
with no-one left at home I had no choice.
My tasks are much the same, to cook and clean,
but there are stairs, and windows made of glass,
bedrooms with hearths – a fire in every one
a luxury that I can scarce believe,
and I must carry coal and tend them all.
The house is warm. I've food enough to eat,
but all day I'm alone, and how I miss
those early days at home, the company –
my mother, brother, sisters, most of all
the wee one always asking what and why.
Instead of chatter, endless thud of pumps,
harsh warning shouts that make me catch my breath
and dread the worst until the blast has passed.
I hear the crack and fall of broken rock.
I feel the slate floor shake beneath my feet
and fear, one day, the isle will split in two
and Belnahua sink beneath the waves.
I steal a moment, stand beside the door,
longing for springs of water, fresh and sweet,
South Uist breezes, white shell sands of home;
but all I find is dust and tainted air,
gunpowder smell, and endless, endless slate –
no space for machair flowers, no skylark song.

Mavis Gulliver

Christina MacDonald from South Uist appeared in the 1881 Census as a domestic servant employed by Angus Shaw, Belnahua Quarry Master, to keep house for him and his 19 year old son.

The Wake

You must put it behind you
someone said –
like the wake that swallowed my daughter.

When they wrapped her up
in a canvas bag,
placed her into my arms,
she was the weight
of a bundle of washing;
her small body
stitched into the sailcloth.

On night watch, time of sea burials
I softly laid her on the deck;
the doctor said some prayers;
I wore my Sunday dress
and bonnet to see her off.

The captain swung the lantern
under a band of stars
as they lowered her down
to the foaming flowers –
waves which would beat
the fever from her, waves like
creamy clusters on the rowan tree at home.

Even the crew cried
for the un-lived life of my child.
Marianne, Marianne, I called,
and the wind carried her name away.

Denise Bennett

The ship *North* sailed from Ireland to Australia in 1883; six children died on the three month voyage.

Road to the French Border, 1939
after a photograph by Robert Capa

Here is a child I know.
He can slip over the border
in his overcoat and blanket.

How can he make a shadow
in these bearing-away hills?
What belongings can he have

here where the trees are so uneasy,
so at a distance?
Wherever I go I see him

along the road from Barcelona.
He is the one I rush back to
in the first light, before anyone is awake,

his bed stripped, the cloistering shutters.
Keep going, keep going I whisper.

Jane Duran

Magadan

On days when birds fell
from the sky like hailstones
frozen by the air itself

the sun was so small
it was as if it didn't know
how to warm the earth any more.

In all that whiteness they set out
past the fence, towards the empty plain
to pull beetroots from the hard ground.

On cold nights, as we burrow
under down, it seems
an indulgence to think of them

but I see their footprints in and out
of the perimeter. Follow them
as they're marched again

to lie next to each other
on wooden pallets. And what else
except this thought –

retrograde comet, its heat lost
in all that distance, the flare of its tail
still bright enough to be visible –

what else can I send back to them?

Maria Jastrzębska

Magadan: a town in the Kolyma region of Russia built in the 1930s by slave labour
which became the main transit centre for Gulag deportions.

Where Did They Go?

Where did they go, the unshakeable ones?
The lost ones, last ones,
wound up in the barrier trees.

After the camps at Argelès-sur-Mer,
St Cyprien, at Barcarès, after the barbed wire
in what places did they choose
or not choose to live, upstairs rooms
so swept by roads and travelling?

I have seen these faces swept across pages,
the stepping forward, the leaning of the body forward
at the border, in the wind. What languages
did they find their timid way among?

What streets did they find to live in,
cities with streets to throng in?

Jane Duran

this is called escape

.

Our Dream

We knew, of course, the journey would be long
and dangerous, my mother old and frail,
the children trusting, so that it seemed wrong

to put their lives at risk when we set sail
in this old overloaded rubber boat
which took on water, forcing us to bale

with just one plastic pail to stay afloat.
The wind was rising, no stars in the sky
to guide us on to Lesbos, so remote

and as we huddled close the waves grew high
crashed down and flipped us over with a swirl,
flung many to the depths and some to die –

for here we lost our precious baby girl.
But strong arms pulled me, mother, son and wife
to safety – shaking, grieving for our pearl.

So now we're in a camp, a dreary life,
long queues for food, not knowing when we'll leave,
my mother sick, for cholera is rife –

but still we dream of peace, we still believe.

Jean Watkins

No-one's Son

You keep moving, a prayer-wheel
in moon shadow, owl-light. A melancholy
funambule, a nightjar, you cross
a northern plain. This is called escape.
You learn rails, roads, waves, aircraft roar.

Today in flint flatlands
no mother mountain looks down.
No friendly hills, those aunts
and grandmas with rounded shoulders,
keeping an eye on you. You miss them.
You are filius nullius, unseen, one
who finds danger in progress.

Where is home? Heartache in a haunted
landscape. Where are you going?
Things were stolen from your childhood.
Now you search for missing pieces
of yourself. You are a collection of warped
bones holding shells for sea sounds.

Jenny Morris

The Blanket

Cold, yes, under a sodium sky at three o'clock in the morning.
But there's this shawl to wear and tea with Manuka honey

and across the only gap in the border, a thousand refugees an hour
pouring through Ras al-Jedir. An hour? By morning, my morning,

another five thousand, by lunchtime, another five and how many
have even a striped hemp blanket? Fifteen thousand blankets!

Imagine one. The way it folds stiffly as a tent around the head
bent back, the shoulders jutting, knees drawn up, wrists free,

the lone triangular edifice. Feel the weave. Hairy, ridged.
Smell it. Determine the sightlines either side of the hollowed cheeks.

Imagine the scene in silence, not as it would be. The blanket
as a block, a wood carving. The tools: straight gouge, spoon gouge,

back bent, dog leg, fishtail chisels, V-tools, punches, vices;
hook knives, drawknives, rasps and rifflers, mallets, saws, abrasives;

slip waterstones – how quiet they sound – and strops for sharpening.
Figure in a blanket. In acacia, sycamore or, most likely, olive.

Mimi Khalvati

37

As Insubstantial as the Suitcase

As insubstantial as the suitcase
in the hand of this refugee chasing his dream, hesitating,
the stork's nest loose in the wind on the boundary
where thoughts alter, bringing his alien brood,
so close to his childhood's river he could spit
across, examined by this Czec Officer,
his throat cannot define sounds.

He had not expected to see this. His dreams have not yet
caught up with unpacking. Open up, says this Officer,
in polished bright uniform, smile and split shoes.
This refugee with sore feet, wife and children
clamouring like storks, the nest floating
downstream behind him, falters.

On his wife's face the translucence of frost. The surface
hangs from his cardboard suitcase. He undoes
the uneven buckle. This suitcase has been
through three uprisings, it's his life.
His son has his stork feather inside,
the strap has frayed at the end.

He opens his suitcase. This air, this dwindling river
cannot harm. Customs will not unpack this
blurring of wings scattering snowstorms.
He almost drops his folded documents,
unearthing double headed eagles.
Customs must let them return.

His mouth is dry as the air in his suitcase. He coughs,
thinking of aunt's pork dripping. How can he hope
to retain the childhood dreams of his country.
He thinks of the stork following her nest
bumping onto the shore, caught up
by a branch.

He has to wait,
has to walk up the stony street with his white-faced family,
pass the tall gates, the cross, the white church walls,
his family linden tree, enter the shuttered house,
the inner courtyard. If the Officer unpicks
patchwork documents, let the stork
beat her avalanche of wings.

Valerie Bridge

Leaving Czechoslovakia, 1964

When we reached the border
in her small red Trabant
our cases were lighter: the pleated dresses,
jeans we'd given to aunts and nieces;
our footsteps behind us on the mountain
where we walked with her family
up towards the border with Poland,
our plimsolls wet, our hair lank from drizzle;
sweet and savoury Knedlicky we'd eaten;
songs we'd sang, drunk on vodka,
already flown, small skittering birds;
the yellow Objizdka sign in Prague diverting us
into the path of a funeral, black plumed horses.
The border guards with their guns gather
around us as we try again to open the boot,
our stiff smiles telling us not to think
of the airmail letters for America
hidden under the back seat.

Fokkina McDonnell

On a Road near Koronovo
for Vera Forster

Shots from behind, the guards prodding them
with the butts of their guns, how they tried
not to look at one another, dragged
their feet like sleepwalkers, along a road

lined with bystanders, the way a woman in a fur coat
reached out to turn her small daughter round,
buried the child's face against her, *for we were not*,
she says, *a sight for a child.* She remembers

when it began to snow, how Gerda in front slipped,
was not helped – the others would grab your coat
if you bent down to help – and once down,
you could not get up. And when she knew the march

could go on forever and ever, that the highway had no end,
there was a scuffle at the back, a stepping aside, and
a girl on a bicycle who must have ridden after them
all the way from the last town; the snow crunching

under her tyres, as slowly, cleverly, she swerved between
the staggering women, spoke to them in ice-puffs,
keep going, the Russians are catching up with you,
keep going, just ten kilometres, don't give up.

The women thought the guards would shoot her,
her flying coat an easy target, but in a breath her bicycle
veered off down a country lane and out of sight
as their army of ragged skeletons came to life,

began a dogged shuffle towards Koronovo. She cannot
recall the face of the girl, though she's tried
all her life, just the sound of her fearless young voice,
the snow, as it settled on her short fair hair.

Wendy Klein

Refugees

When do we leave –
Cancel the milk, stop the papers?
There are whispers on the train
And letters go astray.
We are not wanted here.

Once, we were decent folk,
Growing a little stout,
Respecting the law and the neighbours.
We cast our vote, when we remembered,
And forgot it decently afterwards.

Now waiters refuse to serve us
And the school has no places.
The man on the street shouts hate
Not news, and our parties are invaded
By black-shirted men.

Perhaps we should pack our cases.
But where should we go? And how?
The wind blows cold across the station.
Who would want us, anyway –
Decent folk, growing a little stout?

Pauline Kirk

Roots

A small brown boy,
a sulky underlip,
eyes darting,
little fish in shallows.
Luggage,
his almost memories
on his back,
a passport, bought
at great expense.
He's legal, sort of.

She never understands
why he screams to see
the flowers of flame
in the Christmas grate,
why he still wets the bed,
how, green as the leaves
on cloth his mother sold
at market is not the same
as English green
that mists spring trees,
is fragile as a fistful of sky
and sky is thin blue
milk and scalded cream.

He never understands
how she was cracked,
not broken, emptied out,
except and if,
only his crumpled fist
would open for her.

They never understand.
But knit one, pearl one,
who knows what grows,
or may, from their tangled skein of roots?

Kate Foley

Dislocation

Somewhere in my mind, at my shoulder
he's still there; that pause he takes
on the edge of a rocky path
forcing itself up the grim slap
of a wintry mountain.

His jacket's too big, woollen,
twenty years out of fashion
a man's jacket – bleached grey
like the sky and the low clouds.
He's going to be tall, but his body
still has that soft outline,
that tender plumpness
boys have – just before they grow.

His mother climbs ahead of him
holding tight to a little one.
It's sleeting on their bundled lives.

He stops, looks back at what's below
whatever is left. Even from this distance
of camera lens – and the miles between –
I can see, more clearly than I'd choose,
he hates that he is crying.

Sheila Templeton

Pressure and Displacement

Some sounds I will never forget.
A helicopter landing in the high street,

the crowd's hush, hope gripped tight
to a plastic carrier bag, the unexploded weight

of silence, the whole town tight-lipped.

But the chatter of sparrows in a radio report
from Afghanistan doesn't seem right.

Here is dappled shade and water I don't expect,
normality in the aftermath of a drone attack.

The birds are too cheerful and bright.

And yet small things can and do defy terror.

A refugee camp of several thousand or more.
Every day they come. From the air

they seem like branching streams that pour
into one river. The border

that dams them won't hold them forever.

They will find a way – must find it – and enter.
The miracle is this – laughter

as children cluster round the reporter,
how fear alone might not shape their future.

Pat Winslow

Home

for Tom

How beautiful you are when you do not understand me.

I turn on my heel, remembering, say 'I will see'

and, in my mind's ear, hear my old asylum-seeking Fetle say

'I back, I back'.

Back from her own far country

where she wasn't detained

and didn't die.

Gillian Allnutt

Not Belonging

His eyes plead not belonging
among the women:

the grandmothers shawled in grief,
their daughters suckling infants
born on the bitter mountain.

His bruised eyes claim manhood
no less than father, brother, uncle, cousin,
taken to the place of mounds
and ditches.

Smudged cheeks betray his childhood
among the women,
the grey-faced women,
the shamed men too old to hide in the forest,
the boys too young to leave their sisters.

He defies anyone to accuse him of survival
among those who know no more belonging,
who will one day make children
without grandfathers
in a strange land.

Elisabeth Rowe

ask me about home

Cabbage Cutters Wanted. Basic English. Night or Day.

I am observing how they stand, graphite dark
and neat as knitting in the distant field;
wondering how so many can be so one,
and I think – cabbage?

Next time I'm scratching my own patch,
I'm thinking seeds, cabbage – and the men
who come from far away for nothing much,
and find nothing much,
and are out there now, lopping splattered leaves,
slashing at stalks, up to here in mud.

So when I spot some cabbage, unregarded
on the grass shelf, I understand
it's a serious business, and I choose carefully,
as if they were not all the same,
as if they were not the food of last resort.

And now I have chosen. I have carried it home.
I am squeezing the plump heart,
admiring the slick sheen
of the common or garden, astonishing cabbage.
My fingers slip over satin leaves
purple and petrol blue; I note
how the white veins spread from the stalk
into the filigree end of things;
the weighty roundness making me think of
pregnant bellies or severed heads
and how the smell of it isn't of bedsits or hostels,
but open air and desperate men, longing for home.

Ann Alexander

Casualty

Who are you, bundled on the sidewalk
like household rubbish?

I am nothing
debris of an ordinary day

What were you,
under this sun which does not forgive,
under this sky which does not weep?

I was a strong hand waving
a mother's kiss
a child's running feet

Why did you stay here in the killing city
after the soldiers came?

My home is here
my father's father's home.
I speak with the city's voice

How shall I mourn you
how remember you?

Do not shed tears.
Their bitter salt
rusts all bright hopes

Do not sing funeral hymns
their cadences fall heavy

Do not bring flowers
their petals spill

Give me a shape,
a human shape again
build me in words
name me

A C Clarke

See p.159 for versions in Scots & Gaelic.

Asylum

I ask you about home
and you tell me
home is where the river runs
home is where the dates grow
in bunches
and dry, brown in the sun
home is where your father
farms the land
and drives his horses
home is where you have a father
or did have.
I ask you where you come from
and you say
I come from here.
Here is where I'm from
no back story
no foreigner's tale
because only strangers are foreign
and I am not strange
I am human
like you.
You ask me how I spend my days
and my nights
and I tell you
I spend my days thinking
and my nights
writing poetry
in a dark place
so I can try to imagine
what it is like
to leave prison behind in one country
only to arrive in another
the next.
You ask me about home
and I tell you.

Cheryl Moskowitz

53

Ghost in the Machine

Jack Davis in overalls, wearing a cap
after his day job as a brickie, repairs
secondhand bikes, to earn extra
to pay the mortgage on the house he painted
green, white and yellow, at the time of ads
in corner shops, Rooms to Let, no blacks no Irish.

In the box room of number sixteen, spare wheels
hang from six inch nails, the floor a shingle
of nuts and bolts, the smell of three-in-one oil
heavy as khaki. Hands fretted from wire wool
he polishes aluminium rims to silver, removes
links from the chain until it fits.

His memory full of the sea,
fine tunes into each wave
as if it were the one that broke when he left
a country where there are no words for yes and no.
Sue-Sue Lambert shopping in Dun Laoghaire
meets one of the Davises and asks,
Is Jack not after coming home?

Jo Roach

In Market Street

The men, with moustaches and waistcoats,
smoking strange tobacco, look for a café.
The headscarved women stare at unfamiliar vegetables
and wonder what to make for supper.
An infant sucks a cloth that tastes of home.
Sharp eyed and whip thin children
eye up other children.

The town, smelling of pasties and daffodils,
absorbs them in the mix. It's seen strange before;
Phoenician traders, Spanish invaders,
Welsh miners, Bohemian travellers.
These shy families can rest in the generosity of its indifference.
Lamani or Tregenza, Ionesco or Tresize,
we're all foreign here – or foreign somewhere.

Liz Woods

Son of the Mother-whose-children-are-like-fish

At 19, the mouth of the Ogun breathes him out,
the Humber inhales him, but it's the Aire,
that slithers through his sharp-dressed dances;
his college rejection; his Labour Exchange queue;
that (once Tetley'd) slakes his foundry heat.
Ellerker and Kitching are going white
stomping him through Allport's five stages.
The Loiner rain finds him wandering abroad
in 'the jungle' of Middy Woods, shop doorways,
Armley nick, Millgarth nick, the Dark Arches.
It's Mire Beck that circles his corridor-slur of High Royds
where friends hold him, and the nurse chaperones his hand
dipping to the water-blue airmail *Owon baba… Owon Yemoja…*
And then it's Stage 5 and the long-stanked Aire holds him under.
But PC Galvin blows his whistle, Philips writes 'Lame Darkie',
Sandford's 'Smiling David' speaks from British wirelesses
and when the 30-year-gag coughs out police charge sheets
marked 'Wog' it releases a rush of art and outrage that keeps
David alive. Here he is, age 86. And in his garden
we hold him, hear his quick laugh.

Char March

Immigrant

At the flower stall on the corner
things have all the look of spring,
those tender colours
and such scents
but a broken crust of leaves
across the pavement
where pigeons beak for charity,
the sun's pale face
and a slight huskiness in the light
insist upon December
while below ground
a cold wind blows from the tunnel
a chill miasma of grease, dust
and stale urine grabs the throat
and stings the eyes
so that at first I do not see him
lying there
under a shroud of blankets,
still, monumental,
embalmed in sleep
but then as I approach him
he stirs and rears up from his rags,
start-eyed as Lazarus, haloed
by wild black hair
and I am stopped there,
astonished by the whiteness
of his skin, smooth and unflawed
as the old woman's lilies,
as the strong shoots of plants
that push through stones
towards good air.

Angela Kirby

Two Old Black Men on a Leicester Square Park Bench

What do you dream of you
old black men sitting
on park benches staunchly
wrapped up in scarves
and coats of silence
eyes far away from the cold
grey and strutting
pigeon
ashy fingers trembling
(though it's said that the old
hardly ever feel the cold)

do you dream of revolutions
you could have forged
or mourn
some sunfull woman you
might have known a
hibiscus flower
ghost memories of desire

O it's easy
to rainbow the past
after all the letters from
home spoke of hardships
and the sun was traded long ago

Grace Nichols

Cocklers

Half dusk. Low water. A frieze
of figures stooping, ankle-deep, dark
on dark, in a slow tide they might have crawled from,
scaly feet and fingers gripping rock.
But these are men, living on the hard tack
of hope, wrenching the tough salt of their wages
– a sea traffic so hidden, for all we know
scrimshaws record its tools and practices.
Methodical as potato-pickers, they bend,
sweep, gather, store, ignoring the web
of cold that gathers between fingers and toes
and the white combs of the waves rolling up

to drown the ribbed tracks to safety. Already
men flounder in the long swell, gulping
the tide until it swallows them, mouths
open in silent Os, bodies turning

cartwheels in the undertow, pulled further
and further on the current's thread, flotsam
that drifts, tumbles, finds the shore too late –
known by a single tooth or a lucky charm.

Christine Webb

Are We Vermin, Mama?

Are we earthworm turning? Shiny
green and red railroadworm, bloodworm
which when it dies in enormous heaps
the smell makes noses wrinkle, inch worm –
it measures new land in loops, then steps
back pretending it's a twig – enchanting
glowworm, mealworm for snacks, Mama,
hard-working silkworm or woolly bear
worm surviving the winters, rolling
into a ball if it's disturbed or picked up?

Mama, are we pigeon, crow, snake,
are we rat? Little mouse, flea, ant? I don't mind
being puma – someone said they saw one – or
red kite, they were nearly extinct, but look
at their long wings, Mama. We could be fox,
even wolf, something that burrows like rabbit
or only eats plants like goat does. But what are they
who call us them when we are us? Clouds
that drift? Particles of dust? Same as us.
To be cherished or lost. No beseeching, Mama.

Maria Jastrzębska

Following the 2016 referendum, police in the UK reported an increase of hate crimes against minority communities. These included attacks on Polish people who were sent messages saying: 'Polish vermin go home'

Dinka Labourers in Khartoum

At dusk they entered the garden
wrapped in their indigo rags, stalking
as delicately as crowded cranes
to join their men,

and crouched under the wall, long limbs
like the folded wings of bats, the glint
of silver at a wrist, the gleam
of downcast smiles,

and lowered slings from their shoulders
to the cool dust. Peeled away cloths. Pot,
sticks, bread, pouch of millet, sleeping
face of a child.

Their words were single twigs, fed in
to the little fire. The men lay still,
picks put by, heads on folded arms;
and then one sang,

perhaps of the price of a bride,
a beaded forehead, flight of a spear,
savour of flesh above the embers,
a humped white bull.

There was the pale gecko pausing
and pausing on the shadowy wall.
and there was the lamp, and the dust
under the lamp,

and the smell of bitter orange
seeping from the dark, and the music
of exile north or south, and loss,
and lack of kin.

M R Peacocke

Minority

'Half the Chinese children who've been educated in Britain
can't speak English when they leave school.'
House of Commons Report, 1990s

I can think in his language
but I refuse to speak it.
He cannot punish me;
my smile is so meek.

He makes
on the chalk board
ugly tumbling words
that hold no pictures.

I know on certain days
the nape of his neck
gets suddenly cold;
he has a headache.

My grandmother has taught me
a massage to cure that.
What foods to eat;
what to avoid.

How can I revere a people
that boils its vegetables
whose skin smells of suet
and Brussels sprouts.

Patricia Pogson

Place

As for words, he used so few
that his past was a high stone wall
leading down to the strand
and the smell of the sea
where fishermen never learned to swim.

He listened to a man from Wicklow play
runaway notes on his fiddle
in Camden Town or Kilburn
where the air was stale
in bars that were not home.

When my father's largeness left him
he went looking for a place to die
within walking distance of the sea
and the shadow of mountains
he could put a name to.

Jo Roach

a path to nowhere

Just Visiting

We visit them, the living dead,
in residential homes
which smell of piss and disinfectant,
where the flowers are plastic
and the carers smile – and smile
and we wouldn't do their job
for all the tea in Tescos –
where the residents sleep
in front of the television,
and my neat aunt sleeps
in a green upholstered chair
as the man next to her
fondles himself
under his tartan blanket,
where a shrivelled leaf of a woman
drifts along the corridors,
fumbling at the locks,
asking a passing nurse
May I go home now? Please open
the door, I should like to go home –
and the nurse steers her
back to her room, saying
This is home now, dear.

Angela Kirby

Memory Ward

you tag along with the chef
to learn how a hundred meals
are served hot and all at once

he takes you to the memory ward
lets you serve the puréed lunch
that looks like scoops of ice cream

and I proffer the vanilla potatoes
pistachio greens and mocha meat
hoping to jolt their memories
of summer and seaside joy
but features remain frozen
as spoons are picked up
and carers tie the paper bibs

Elsa Fischer

Alzheimer's

I'm making fog.
It clogs the names
of faces I can feel
the shape of –
children...grandchildren...

It's cotton wool
at the top of a pill bottle;
I want to tug it out,
touch the shiny beads,
but my fingers won't
do as they're told.

I'm wasp-drunk
in a puddle of jam,
sticky-brained.

Once I tapped buttons
and words covered a sheet.
now he gums labels
to all our things
– chair, cupboard, table –
the man who keeps me.

But my sting's real.
I can read that
in his face.

Patricia Pogson

The Carer

That last fall he had
the one that killed him
left bloodstains on the carpet.
She scrubbed and scrubbed
but still she saw them.
She decided to make a claim.

The assessor called and
saw no evidence.
You shouldn't have
scrubbed it. You should have
left the evidence there for me to see.
Looking through her
breathing shallow, smelling the poverty
I see no evidence, he said.

She felt him look through her
look right through her, and thought
What evidence do you need?
Shall I unbutton my blouse
peel back the skin
let you see the stains
still there
on my heart?

Anne B Murray

Widow's Mite

Standing in the kitchen,
in the one spot that interferes
with everyone else's business,
next to the knife drawer,
in front of the gas oven,
by the cupboard under the sink
where the bleach is kept,
staring helplessly
at a broken glass;

having no opinions,
being of no account,
wanting to do nothing,
stating no preferences,
except perhaps
not eating potatoes,
not liking the hill to the house,
not wanting flowers in the bedroom,
wanting it not to rain;
little remarks – only joking –
like barbs in the skin,
stifled sighs, of disappointment
at the state of the son;

the drift of these small years
silts up and silts up
until the harbour is filled in
and no boat comes.

Yet still the cups of tea,
stockings dripping in the bath,
the straggle of geraniums,
the TV pitched to deaf ears,
habits of boredom
trailing their miserable wake
through half-hearted,
shifting sands.

What's needed to turn
the tide is the will:
the pills in the bathroom cabinet,
the loose bit of carpet
on the dark of the stairs;
or the morse code of
arms flailing SOS.

Rosemary McLeish

Neighbour

In the night
Patsy, at my door, faces me
skin pale and eyes rimmed with white.

At eighty, floating fragile and open,
she expects me to go with her
reluctant, into the night.

She is me, she is you, she is where life leads to.

Three chattering old friends
had pushed into her room.
And, her day usurped,

tossed up to my door – almost
she's blown from her life – asking
take me back, take me back home.

Night, like earth, lies under,
catching the leaves that are blown.

And it is there in her room, pushes
up to her window; the curtains
only partially closing on the night.

The bulb sheds its light. Only
this moment. Old-age bent over –
entwining one love with another.

Take me back, take me back home.
Night is where life leads, like earth,
lies under, catching the leaves that are blown.

Sara Boyes

73

Nervosa

I'm the ultimate artist:
sculptor and sculpted.
I offer my truth
on the bony curve of a parched hip.

Tarzan-like, I swing
sinew to sinew, pull my own strings.
No puppet. The lightness of these limbs
reflects the agile universe I live in.

I'm thinner than my shadow,
can slip between the cracks
like smoke. For me,
no doors are closed.

Butterfly of bravado,
no nectar required,
I'm fuelled by the sweetness
of a different dimension.

Time slides by me.
Count the years
in the bite of each section of spine.
I'm a small tent of sagging skin,

drawing myself
further and further in.
Umbilicus knot imploding,
winching my tongue into darkness.

You cannot
read my eyes,
decode the masterful triumph
of my ever-shrinking smile.

Fiona Durance

See note p. 159.

A Calling

She was a woman. A poor start in life, but you
Can't change that, and you soon learn. Even
As a child she was grown-up, and like a child she

Didn't count. There wasn't much money, so
There weren't many choices. She said yes,
All right, or else just yes. In a mixed class,

The teacher didn't ask her, anyway. Did he
Even know her name? The classroom was
Crammed, and she was always at the back.

The last girl picked for a team, she wasn't
Good at friends. No one tried it on with her,
Or took what didn't happen further.

The telly made it clear it was her spots
(Blemishes, they called them). Or her breath?
She thinks it was her legs perhaps,

But didn't worry much. Being a woman's
All she knows – and what a woman does. She's
Not abused. She's fed. She's got a bed –

She's lucky. Some day someone will get
Something out of her. Things could be worse.

It's just a waste of time to write this verse.

R V Bailey

Lifted

Red scarecrow girl/a slip of a thing
this hollow dried out twig of a thing/blackbird eyes darting
like a Don't Look Now vision/object of derision
caught her on CCTV/this hint of a thing
shivering skin-and-bone stick of a thing
rattling about in a size ten coat/ten sizes too big for her frame.

This man/this guard/this brick of a thing
this thick-skinned/hard-nosed prick of a thing
sausage pink fingers came right up behind her
grabbed her shoulder like porcelain china
such a fragile delicate chip of a thing.

The room where they took her/a pit of a thing
windowless/nowhere-to-sit of a thing
they poked and they prodded and picked at the girl
said they'd call the police and tell all the world
what a low-down/uncivilised trick of a thing
and she shook.

This creature/this bird/this wishbone-thin little flit of a thing
featherless/fatherless spit of a thing
she blanked all the voices and fingers and pointing
she left them all there with their out-of-nose jointing
and flew from the room through the back of her mind
this practically invisible/wholly derisible
breakable/shakable/bit of a thing.

Cheryl Moskowitz

76

Bride's Story

I came here because he said he loved me.
He married me, didn't he? It was a surprise
the first time he hit me but I deal with it,
go numb, show no fear, never cower.

I don't cry anymore. I want to leave
but there are no bus stops here.
I could walk along a path to nowhere
but the grass is high, animals prowl.

By day I sit in this clearing beside the hut,
peer at orange dust. At night gekkos
walk on suckered feet above my head
and I'm so scared they'll fall.

I dream of cold winds, grey skies,
and damp tenement walls.

Eveline Pye

Under the Mubaba Tree

She walks away from the giant grinding bowl,
wilts against the mubaba tree,
her back on the trunk, legs apart
head falling forward, too tired to swat the flies.

Her third daughter was delivered
into disappointed hands. She remembers
his face turning away, the next day
her battered suitcase left on the stoep.

His mother held onto Mosa and Luata
and their screams faded slowly
as she began the long walk back
to the village where he found her.

Eveline Pye

Mubaba: African dry zone mahogany
Stoep: verandah or covered porch

A Short Chapter in the History of Stone

Small girls play in the shadow of mud brick walls.
A pile of jackstones flips from grubby palm
to sharp knuckle.

Dreaming, nursing stone babies –
some have gold flecks in their round heads,
like the sun in a pail of water.

Pebble in a first pair of grown-up
shoes. His parents. Yours. You kick off the hot
fidgety shoe secretly under your robe.

Your brother burns flags. Throws unerring stones
at embassy cars. Skips home
like a young goat.

Your first child is a girl.
You make a leaf bracelet
for her chubby wrist.

Not very old yourself
you try to soften the rock-hard disapproval
of your not very old husband

who will never believe
his sperm has selected two
baby girls.

One burnt supper. One tearful wife
runs from the compound leaving a smell
of scorch in the air,

holds her swollen cheek, trips on a stone,
falls in the gravelly dust, is lifted
by a friend of her brother,

who runs his thumb gently over her eyelids.
The rest will soon be history
written by stone.

Kate Foley

As I Remember

The bamboo ferry slip
stands lopsided in the water,
an outpost of the village
growing old; the shallows
lap against the pilings.

Grateful for a breeze
the sampan
with its turquoise sail
gets up speed, sails
past the sunset.

But on the beach
in ribboned light, a small girl
kneels to stop our path.
I give good massage, she says.
Any kind you want, I have.

Josie Walsh

Morning Men

They sit on park benches,
hands clasped between knees,

staring ahead, or down at their feet
where smashed glass, fag ends, spilled

Chinese, feathers – the remains of a kill
in the dark or a just-quick-enough flight,

lie quiet among leaves, the night's
noises over. The sun's warm for October.

One West Highland White chases another,
running flat out, in the moment, forever.

These men are on hold, some never
sure what a walk home will bring –

dust gathering on shelves, a ring
left on a dresser, stained mugs in the sink,

the TV still blinking.

Geraldine Paine

Easter

Outside the library
the old drinkers rock
and hug themselves,

crying softly, cursing,
and the snow falls
in slow motion

through the bloom
of a flowering cherry.
April showers.

A man stumbles
on his wavy line
across ground that glitters,

his tread crunching
snow crystals, broken glass
and white petals

that bruise to a faint
pink smear behind him,
as if he walked barefoot.

Sheenagh Pugh

The Drunken Chiel Chats ti the Muin

Whit ir yi daein
hingin aboot in the skeh
wi a smile on yir fizog
as wide's the Forth?

An aa thae wee staurs
dancin roonaboot,
fireflehz skinklin in the mirk,
trehin ti ootdae ain anither.

Tap doag Sirius
baits them aa
fir luminositie.
He's a bona fide dehmond.

Fran Baillie

Competitor

As for what I could have been – well, I could
have danced into the dawn. My little feet
would have outspun all others. How they would
have outflung the rest of them, sweet and fleet
with delight. I could have quick-stepped as fast
as life, footloose – look! – as the final shower
of gold melting into the arms of last
light. Light thoughts. Long evening. Even hour.

So it's too late to compete. My brief time
for winning praise has run out. No-one asked
for my hand (or saw my great grief). No-one,
I think, knew I was waiting. Now that I'm
away from the dance-floor (untried, unrisked)
I go slow. One. Two. Soon I will have gone.

Helena Nelson

all those back-breaking months

Night Nurses in the Morning

No bench in the bus shelter; they slump
against caving perspex, dragging the Silk Cut

deep into their lungs, eyes closed, holding
the moment, then letting a long breath go.

And they don't talk. Swollen ankles above
big white boat-shoes, dreams of foot-spas.

Pale pink pale green pale blue, even without
the washed-out uniforms you could tell them

from us other early-morning faces
going in, starting the day. We eye them sideways

as they fall into seats, ease their shoes off.
More pallid than colliers or snooker players,

the vampires of mercy. All their haunts lie near
this bus route: here's St Stephen's Hospice,

where folk go to die; there, the Lennox Home
for Elderly Ladies. Just round the bend,

the other granny-park, where I walked past
an open window one evening when the lilac

was out, and heard a young voice scream, over and over,
You bitch, you bitch, and another tone

querulous and high, a complaining descant
to her theme. They both sounded desperate.

People who live by night aren't quite canny.
We let them keep things running, avoid their eyes,

resenting the way they don't seem to need us there.
What do you do, in the corners of darkness

where we sweep the inconvenient? What is it
you never say to each other on the bus?

As our faces wake, exhaustion silvers
the backs of their eyes: not windows but mirrors.

Sheenagh Pugh

Cultivators

We,
who work with earth and steel
and feel winter frozen in our hands
where fields are looms,
weave the patterns of crops;
damp loam flows like silk
through shuttling metal.

And our hills,
with their wild uncurbable wills,
may be hard to till
but are easy to love;
steep work weakens the tractor
but strengthens the heart.

Susan Taylor

The Florist's Assistant

Each day her fingers bleed from picking thorns from
long-stemmed roses, for the sake of other people's
lovers, mothers; she takes her time to bruise and crush
the woody stalks of hothouse blooms, then strips the leaves
below the water line, takes tweezers to remove
each less than perfect petal, every bud gone blind.

For the gone but not forgotten, the sadly missed,
belov'd in this life, cherished in the next,
she stands on wet stone flags and leans her body
up against the workbench while she wires and hammers,
twists and binds, inhales chrysanthemums gone over,
day-old lilies and the fumes of waterlogged gypsophila.

Susan Utting

Coast

They call it paradise, this land
that bled us dry – fanning
our burnt-out pride. But paradise

is for the dead. Let them try
as we did, squandering their young muscle
damming, digging trenches, laying drains –

let them winch nags up cliffs
or starve, wrestle mudslides, drought and flood –
and in a few years let them sicken

of the same few family names,
congenitally careworn faces.
Let them cultivate their feuds

in the same dog-stinking village haunts,
under the same peeling paint.

They call it paradise, this ache
of blue-white sky and mountain,
raising their eyes from pools and paperbacks –

then step out young, sun-stunned,
more wealth in their backpacks
than our hearths ever saw. So let them buy

our ruinous old barns and let us go –
up along the valley over that first col
whose angles spell out life and money

clear as Hollywood. We will find a land
that does not fight us. Mind your backs.
We will phone. We will send money.

Let us pass. Let them
make those stony fields pay.

Julia Deakin

The Blue Lonnen

The crunch of mussel shells under the boot heel;
The bramble-patch where the cottages were rooted;

The stone ring of the mussel bed, the stair
To the drying-green, the ballast heap, the beach of creeve-stones;

The tarry stain where the bark-pot reeked; the wicket
In the wall; on the bridge to the limpets, the blade-worn groove;

The iron pin that marks the sea-road to the haven;
The nail driven into the door jamb – they are illegible

Without the rudder and the anchor,
Without the twine, the needle and the knitter:

For these are the paths they beat to the shore – The Nick.
                              The Blue Lonnen –
And each is a road with a boat at the end of it.

Katrina Porteous

Bark-pot: outdoor pot used to boil tannin-rich bark or 'cutch' to preserve fishing gear.
Creeve-stones: stones used as weights in crab and lobster pots.
Lonnen: lane.

Wicket: small gate.

Chill Factor

He tries to dream cool – of ponds he dared to step on
till he heard the gun-shot crack, stilled waterfalls
in Cumbria, of sleeping in an igloo or an ice hotel.

Sangin dust grits between his teeth, chafes
his shoulder blades, sticks to his sweat no matter
how much care he takes undressing, shaking out.

His final tour. It's 48 degrees: he must think cool –
frost fairs on the Thames, blue light of glacier caves,
Shackleton's *Endurance* trapped and crushed.

Heat beats at his helmet like a welder's torch,
his nape's on fire, eyes sear with watching
as the search team makes its slow way back.

His last long walk. The escort's guns are poised.
Without his body armour he steps light
along the track. Tomorrow – home, to stars

in their proper places, Cathy's frown, the garden
gossipy with birds, the children's bikes to fix.
Soft-fingered sun. Rain. He lies flat, tools

to hand. The silence grows. Now he believes
cool – in Saturn's rings, the Skaters' Waltz,
a white bear on its lonely floe. He wipes his mind,

strokes away sand and earth, starts to unpick
a knotted mass of metal, batteries and wires.
The desert holds its breath.

Gill Learner

The Winchman on Oscar Charlie

I'd like to be the winchman on Oscar Charlie,
if I weren't afraid of heights and helicopters:
lift people lightly from a pitching deck,
head through the dark to Christmas-blazing oil-rigs,
see from high up, so often, I'd almost forget
to take notice, porpoises leaping, the shadows of orca.

I met his mother-in-law at a bus stop once,
the winchman. She told me his working day
you wouldn't believe, the things he'd seen and done,
when now and again she could make him talk about them,
but there was the rub. He wasn't a talking man;
he was strong, fearless, fantastic head for heights,

and he could have filled volumes with the way
he lived the world, the betweenness, sea and sky,
land, deck and platform, that rope, danger and safety,
if he knew the words that would make them happen
for the likes of us, checking our shopping lists,
wondering why the 9.20's late again.

Sheenagh Pugh

Keeping the Light

Mary A. Israel was assistant lighthouse
keeper at Point Loma, San Diego 1873-1876

She gazed up into the snail curl of stair
where shadows had fossilised;
light moved to the waltz of the wind
her needles were purling patterns of ocean.
She was chained into her knitting
starved of the company of women
longing to dine on small gossip
to scallop the edge of their dialogue.

Her bones had stiffened to the beechwood chair
two o'clock chill silhouetted her shape
her hands looked stunted as her mother's.
She kept the ships company, ebbed on their tide
kept her rebellious thoughts as surreptitious
as her tomato plants their growing;
she shook free her cramped limbs
mixed into misty window reflections.

The moon cruised huge with harvest
obscured by soft fibrous film.
Ships were skeining the rollers
tacking between needles of rock.
She shuffled her chair in chalky light
cast off her shawl of cloud, listened
to her needles weaving and the siren stars;
she was forever on watch.

Margaret Speak

The Psalm of Those who Tend the Flocks

They are patient with the wilful ways of the sheep,
for they panic and run the wrong way,
they are confident in their grabbing of the horns,
and the way they can fling them to the ground without harm.
They are watchful with their knowledge for they know
that if a sheep can find a way to die it will,
and they know that while all of them look much the same,
sheep have their own particular natures.
And they are out in the cold and their hands are red,
they are out in the wind and their eyes are watery,
and in the dawn of a spring morning they go out on the hill
and they anoint the new lambs with iodine.
And their dogs are an extension of their will,
whistled up when the sheep are safely penned.
And they live all summer with the call of lamb to ewe,
and they live with the deep bleat of the answer,
and they know all the voices.
And they live by the weathers of the hills.

Jo Peters

Apprentice Cutter
for Jo

She's scared of the women who can put on
their lipstick without a mirror, answer back
full of chelp, while she's fourteen and knows
nothing. Toilet breaks are timed but the work
is a way to some glamour – like in the pictures

where starlets lounge in swaying marabou.
The Kathleens, Dollies, Dots, with swollen feet,
deft hands above the drop feed, zip along
a double French seam, set a sleeve just right
and there's magic in that. She shakes out cloth,

spreads it, makes a snip and rips across
the warp. With tailors' chalk, she snicks darts,
cuts notches to match so collars sit flat
on collar bones. Bent forward, wielding both
plain and pinking shears, her wrist soon sports

a ganglion. Hers is a world of pins stuck in
and forgotten, of bias cut, stretch and pucker,
of slip or bulk jamming under the needle.
From eight till six she cuts out evening blouses,
walks home to save the fare for velvet gloves,

a fold of voile hidden in her bag. She dreams
of devoré, guipure, silk charmeuse; sleeping,
measures yards from nose to fingertip,
the fabric's drop brushing her pretty feet:
picqué, organza, crêpe de Chine, georgette.

Kathy Pimlott

My Shirt

Blue threads link women.
In Bangladesh she wears
a bright sari of thin poor cloth

her hands move swiftly
across bleached denim
so little time lost

so little fuel or coin
needed for her quick work
in dusty slatted light.

My shirt is nothing to her
mere stuff of work work
trance of work as quick quick

through her fingers
she draws seams, tosses garments
into piled baskets at her feet.

Blue blue – she must dream
of blue – such foreign blue –
does she wonder, turning

first sleeve, second sleeve,
folding both sleeves, what other
woman's arms will slide

into this blue – no time
to raise her eyes
to wonder how, and who?

Martha Street

Tom Makes His Mark

Thomas Clarke, Plumber and Glazier
July 4th – 1794, aged 15

I did it for a dare and to win a girl. She said
I never would but I proved her wrong,
chose the horse's arse, bottom left
on the last panel, the one about the apocalypse.

I've a handsome hand but big and this
was the widest expanse of clear glass to write on.
I was proud of my curled initial, though my hand
shook a little when I heard the master coming
and the writing slopes downhill
to the right like on the board at school.

Anyway, after all those back-breaking months
of grozing, of staining my fingers
with lunar caustic and Cousin's rose,
of straining my eyes repainting chain mail,
an ape's tooth, the turned-down mouth
of a knight, the way I saw it, I'd a right.

And who was to know? Once the panel
was hoisted into place and the scaffolding
removed no-one would see the details
till dirt and damp and loosening glue
had undone our handiwork and that
wouldn't be for a century or two.

I like to think of an apprentice
all those years hence, reading my words.
I wish I could tell him about the night,
oh the night, I spent with the girl.

Carole Bromley

Hurdle-maker

I take the cart to the heath
for hazel boughs,
then to the river,
cut willow withies.
My errands of mercy.

I lay my hazels, man length,
weave withies, bind tight.
My works of mercy.

They must be strong,
my hurdles,
my cradles of mercy.

I called our daughter Mercy.
Born a few summers past,
not like me,
she's a one for talk.
Sets herself down in the yard
to watch my merciful work.
Leaves off trailing fingers
in shavings,
points at hurdles
stacked by the wall,
demands: what for?
She'll not understand
my woven work of mercy
for the soon to be dead.
God help me –
To take sick people to the monks
is what I said.

Jo Peters

Hurdle: A kind of frame or sledge on which traitors used to be
drawn through the streets to execution.

Grace Before Meals

She grates beeswax, mixes in turpentine,
then rubs with pads of rags the lobby tables
till khaya wood drowns under shine

like water beneath ice. She spells out labels
for supper; scrapes grease drips from the glass
bowls of hurricane lamps; checks air timetables

for new arrivals. She picks three-awned grass
for the pillow gifts of flowers and chocolate;
sweeps mating locusts and a dead springhaas

off the verandah, then changes her tracksuit
for a fresh pressed khanga, and is in place
at lunch, pouring pinotage, serving fruit.

'Does your baby stay in the township, Grace?'
With my sister. I see him each three weeks.
And here, she taps her head, I keep his face.

Marianne Burton

101

Clare

Her long legs scissor, spiral down the pole.
One arm carves space. She's warm flesh round a skewer.
They hunger, drink in skin. Cash burns a hole
in eager trouser pockets. Her allure's
an empty face. Back home, the babysitter
feeds videos and pizza to the kids.
She smiles: a flash of hollowness, dead glitter.
She blinks, their faces grit beneath her lids.
Beyond the lights, the open-mouthed crowd swells.
Blood's up, contempt behind the baying smiles.
She turns her mind to neutral; flexes, smells
escape – *push on* – ten seconds drag like miles.
At last she's done. Quick change, a cab ride home.
Kids safe, she sleeps, clenched like a fist, alone.

Fiona Durance

See note p. 159.

different casualties

Rage

Pity the poor kid
who learns early that

the face at the cot rail
is that of a stranger;

that for ever and ever means
for the time being;

who hoards the fear of
each small leaving

until the whole edifice
of abandonment

falls like a broken sky.
We should not be surprised

when he takes a knife
to our complacency.

Elisabeth Rowe

Electro-sensitive

They could be you:
your wan fatigue,
your headache's red axe.
Dizziness, tinnitus,
your sleep elusive
as a turquoise moon.

They could be you:
exiled from rooms.
Pub, office, café, train.
Lit glades where friends
would gather, lost amber.
Their lives shrink

as routers grow,
microwaves that drill, drill,
no warnings – tablets,
smartphones, cordless –
vipers, hornets,
smart-meter needles.

They could be you:
phosphors, pearls
dashed aside for data-speed.
As profits pour. Adverts roar.
Wireless! Wireless!
Corporate greed.

Lynne Wycherley

Nearly 700 patients struggling with wireless symptoms were found to have
toxic markers and damaged brain blood-flow linked to exposure.
(Belpomme 2016)

Night Shelter

I hold his body like a lover,
half smothering, half covering
with my rough embrace.

Sleeps seeps into him, unlocks
tight limbs, blots out hunger,
memory, pain.

I am worn with his fumblings,
grubby, yet tender. But my touch
can't ease the ache for home.

I hide no disgrace, no outcast
here. These deft, bruised fingers
once rescued, saved.

Around him, others shipwrecked
and waiting. Through loose foldings
I let in day.

Foreign voices, hasty feet,
hands unwinding, see if he's breathing.
Discarded, I fall to the floor.

Berthing. Drink, food, hope
maybe, of something better
than this, thin spread kindness,
uncovered dawn.

Rosemary Doman

They Just Use Dogs to Get Extra Dosh

This is my person
He sleeps beside me

I have had him for two years
I found him in a Waitrose car park

I brought him some newspapers
My person likes newspapers – and cardboard

He gave me a cream cake from the bin
He tied himself to me with this string

This is our home
It glitters with smells

It is best in winter
Then the metal tubes blow hot air

In summer it is cars' barks
And there are loud people

They come and kick my person
They try to kick me

Sometimes he is sick
I usually eat his sick

Then I take him to the big place that echoes
They give him a hot bowl

They give me crunchy bits and a stroke
Then they scare my person with pieces of paper

He takes his cardboard
He takes my blanket

I lead him back home

Char March

Title as heard on a BBC Radio Leeds phone-in about people sleeping rough in the city.

Song of the Stepchild

The village is as perfect
as a snow-globe

On a summer table, a glass bloom
that seems to catch the light

and make it liquid.
Shake it, till snow

lies on imaginary pavements,
on windowsills, and in the sepals

of glass flowers –
There I am at home, there I am

in the lane, there
I am in the classroom –

One day soon I'll break
the glass skin;

as spring rain-storms
shatter the morning.

Fiona Sampson

No Room

He sleeps in a cupboard in a dark flat high up
in a huge city. He wants to launch himself
from a window. Instead he throws out
his plate of saucisson.

He's a small boy always in trouble.
There's no room in his shoes.
Wrong shaped feet. He must have built-up
boots. Hideous, he thinks. He's mocked.

His father doesn't speak the same language.
This foreigner must wait round the corner
every Saturday. Then they go to the park.
The boy likes to trip people up with his boots.

He is sent away as there is no room for him
at home. He stumbles and walks in his sleep.
He sings to himself in his dreams.
He can't find a place to run barefoot.

When he grows up the cupboard will be full
of suitcases. If he can't have a space
in other people's lives he will fly and sing
and they will look up at him and say,
'Now he has all the room he needs.'

Jenny Morris

Bullies

With the eye in the back of his head
he sees them coming –

eight-year-old breakers,
baby-hard, baby-soft.

Their elegant space-machine
could swallow him,

drown him once and for all
in a dish of air.

He freezes
as they expect

though a voice inside him squeaks I . . .
Words cut his tongue,

weigh in his mind
like a bruise.

Katherine Gallagher

Talking Him In Off the Ledge

We all called him Danny Boy – though
That wasn't his name.
And I remember the week it happened –
A lot of thunder that week and old ma Watson hiding
In the coal cellar till it broke.
And then little Danny Boy threatening to kill himself
Though Danny wasn't his given name and
He didn't know what death was.
All he ever wanted was a mam to call his own
And a dad who didn't drink.....
And a bit of jam and bread and perhaps one day
A telly.
I remember it took four hours to get him to come in
And he had started to enjoy it.
I said he could borrow our mam – and that dad would
Fetch him some dandelion an burdock –
But it was when I said he could watch Crackerjack with me
That he came in.
And we stepped over his dad in the hall – a stray dog
At his feet.
Your name's Arthur isn't it, I said – and he smiled.
Hadn't seen him for years until in town the other day.
Pregnant girlfriend towing him along like a truck –
A beer belly protruding under a Superman t-shirt.
How you doing, I asked as he shuffled on past.
'Still on the ledge', he whispered.
'Still on the ledge'.

Helen Burke

Outside

Today I shall not just
watch from the window;
I shall go outside.
Today I'll know
the joy of fine mists combing through my hair,
taste of fresh air, the scent
of rosemary this summer morning.

Today I shall not give in
to the fears that stalk – irrational,
catching breath before I can exhale.
I shall walk away from the window,
wear a blue dress,
pale grey sandals, a cardigan –
nothing to stand out,
nothing to need a second glance.

I shall not turn back
at the front gate,
scurry into the hall.

Today I shall not fear
a neighbour who says hello,
the tabby cat that patrols the wall,
startle of a car horn.

I shall be tall,
breathe deep,
carry a small purse,
a notebook, money.

I'm doing it now,
I'm moving back from the window,
I'm going to walk on grass
instead of looking at it,
going to hear the leaves rustle –
not just watch their movement.
I'm going outside.

Tomorrow I shall go outside.
Tomorrow.

Alison Chisholm

Hush-Hush Girl

Let's hear it for the girl with the
shiny shoes and toes at ten-to-two,
for the bob of her yellow curls,
for her crooked front-tooth gap.

Let's admire the stripes on her palm,
the left-hand devil-possessed one, how
she bit her lip as she smudged and sloped
the wicked way, how she spat and carried on.

Let Miss Meadmore weep for the loss
of her whipping girl, Miss Tolly mourn
a blue serge coat with a twisted belt
and a pair of legs for a flat-hand slap.

I won't let go her crocodile hand in mine,
its grip, the red of its down-to-the-quick;
won't cry out for the hush-hush girl who
went away, for the girl who didn't come back.

Susan Utting

Simpleton

Simpleton, foolish or gullible
simple, pure and simple

soft girl not rough or coarse
quiet and gentle soft in the head.

Cretin from Crestin meaning Christian
feeble minded, touched by god.

Idiot from idio, own, distinct
as in you are your own person.

Dimwit, mental, mental defective
deficiency, handicap cap in hand

crack brained, dolt, dunderhead
maiden, lamb, halfwit, half-baked.

An innocent washed free from original sin
incapable of actual sin.

But everything wasted on earth
is treasured on the moon,

unanswered prayers, fruitless tears
unfulfilled dreams and desires

and you my moon child
my Dowsabell, douce et belle.

Jo Roach

Leros

A white room in a small hotel beside a beach Taverna. Low bed,
thin mattress, cool sheets. Red snapper sizzled on our plates

next to olive oil vegetables and thick white bread. Dogs barked
at night, boats slapped early morning waves. We could choose

where to stay, choose what to eat, choose when to bathe
in the blue Aegean sea.

South on the island we passed the old Institution
grim among trees, where phenothiazine parades replaced

Italian soldiers' marching. Do you remember the photos
and films of three thousand discards from all over Greece?

Empty eyes gazed without connection, knees writhed,
jaws chewed absent mouthfuls; ungainly steps shuffled

down unkempt paths to a room with tables
of old fish stew and dry bread.

In the military Graveyard, planted row on row, stone
by stone, lie different casualties. Do you remember

the Battle of Leros, the last defeat of the British
in World War II, the last German victory?

Now a child on a beach is not playing, a woman
touches her head scarf, a man looks at his feet,

a villager comes with some fish and bread
near a camera that whirrs.

Jane Monach

For decades the most seriously mentally ill people in Greece were sent to the island of
Leros in the Dodecanese. November 1943 saw the devastating end of the Dodecanese
Campaign with great loss of life.

Psychosis

The strange kaleidoscope of her face
turns creakily, caught between pattern and space.
Hands scramble her dress
messy with yesterday's breakfast.
She says she loves dogs who don't like people.
Aristocrat of the odd, she will keep
visitors penned in rerstless
scrutiny until they bore her with niceness,
return her to the sad peculiar people
in her head who complain against each
other, ask her to explain why they are dead.

Patricia Pogson

It Rained All Day

and I thought of him on his own,
how he couldn't pop out to the garden
to check how the plants were getting on.

Instead there would be papers to read
and a fire to light, heavy hours on the sofa
wondering how the spattering and spilling of time
were going to make him whole in the world,

as though gathering ashes and raindrops
in a bowl could be the recipe for goodness,
for knowing who he was.

He'd always hoped his tribe lived by the sea
where there was a different kind of water:
waves that would throw open a vast blue distance,

not this darkening blanket wrapping him into himself.

Susanna Harding

The Boy with a Cloud in his Hand

He hasn't got much: not a roof,
nor a job, nor any great hopes,
but he's got a cloud in his hand
and he thinks he might squeeze
till the rain falls over the town,
and he thinks he might tease
the cottonwool fluff into strands
of thin mist, and blank everything out,
and he thinks he might blow
this dandelion clock so high,
it will never come down, and he thinks
he might eat it, a taste of marshmallow
sliding inside him, filling him up
with emptiness, till he's all space,
and he thinks, when he's hollow and full,
he might float away.

Sheenagh Pugh

sideways into shadow

Headstone

R F White, Musician R.M.B 1893 – 1918
Highland Road Cemetery Southsea

I'm hugging a headstone to-day,
holding a swathe of white paper
rubbing your name in blue crayon.
It comes up R F White RMB 14/12
died aged 25, September 1918.

Your records say you were 4ft 8¾
when you signed up;
grey eyes and brown hair –
learnt clarinet and violin;
no hurts, scars or wounds.

Did you play in the pit at The Kings
on the nights the theatre borrowed
the lads from the band?
A rousing tune perhaps,
or one those old sweet songs
for the girls in the Gods?
Alice Blue Gown,
I'm shy Mary Ellen, I'm shy…

At eighteen promoted to Musician
and Medic, readied for war,
they sent you in *Minotaur* for duties at Jutland:
ship's chapel on Sundays, concerts,
sick berth attendant in combat –
your red hands winding
the bandages…

…and when you came home,
with bubbling lungs those rasping sounds
drowning out your breath –
when you could neither hold a note
or hold a bow –
they wrote down *pneumonia.*

Then your widowed mother
covered you up in earth
and they called your name
Richard Frederick White
one last time.

Under Italian marble now
you lie with other musicians,
to the rumble of buses,
in scattered plots and numbered rows,
allotted like theatre tickets –
your single billet of grass GL6 19.

Denise Bennett

Miss Hathaway Sweeps Her Path in Autumn 1916

'If the women in the factories stopped work for twenty minutes, the Allies would lose the war'. *Field Marshal Joffre*

She sees they have scattered gold where the gate once hung
to tempt her from the path

to tempt her to cross the cracks they even placed a black cat
beyond the boundary

she knew safe. She will not sing though they call her canary.
Her yellow hand swoops

a feather from the path to sweep the gold to shelter by the blind
daffodils, bound since March

when they pretended dead – fallen innocents in a time where diatribe
reigns and generals

remain at the rear. She recognises each passing person's greeting
knowing the code:

a hand half-raised – the salute – the head inclined to the left
– the warning –

or a nod which means she must leave within the week. Speech
is not exchanged.

When he who comes with words lingers where brambles guard the
                                                                      path
she will close the air

where the gate once hung. If the time prove auspicious she will pluck
a snowdrop to light her way.

Ruth O'Callaghan

i.m. the women 'canaries' who suffered mental and physical problems due to the toxic chemicals they worked with in the factories

Eighty Dead Women

here is a walking stick
a scuffed handbag
house keys
worry beads
a bright blue clothespeg
three pairs of scissors

and eighty dead women

seismograph scrawl traced
across the rockface's deep
                    -grooved dry cheeks
ghosts of women
grey-black like buzzards seen
through your eyelashes
in front of the sun

unleashed against the mountain, rising
from the ditch-dust blown over their bodies
by a wind that cries horror
                    cries shame

Mandy Macdonald

On the discovery in November 2015, in the Sinjar mountains of north-western Iraq, of
two mass graves containing the bodies of older Yazidi women

Puzzles

As she speaks, the pretty curve
of her upper lip lifts
as if to smile. And surely
her soul can't help but want
to smile, and skip, and forget
and be six years old.

But already the lip comes down
and closes softly, firmly. Closes on
too much knowledge: about bombs,
how they batter your eardrums,
what the world looks like
after, where the street used to be.

She understands danger – to herself,
her mighty mother, the big kind brother
whose life slips sideways into shadow
hour by hour. The journalist asks how
she gets through it. That nearly smiling lip
lifts again. 'I do puzzles.'

Stevie Krayer

Collaboratrice

I can't say anything against him.
He was kind.
And heavy with the thought
of going home.

I didn't want him to be killed.

It had to be kept
secret. We met at night.
When it snowed
he would make me
walk in his footprints.
Like the page and Wenceslas.

I don't know whether he was killed.

I still would like to see him
if alive.
Only to look –
he's surely got a wife
and children now. It wouldn't do
to interfere.

Well yes – they did. The Résistance.
They shaved my head.
It was to be expected. I don't think
of it now. Much.
The crowd was worse - they set
each other off.
I lived. Some didn't.

But no-one forgets.
There's still a coldness
when newcomers to the village
find out.

When anyone asks whose
is my daughter
I say
she's mine.

Joy Howard

From a Channel 4 interview with three women 'collaborators' from WW II

Katya

Not of my own choosing
do my paps darken like muzzles.
My belly slowly swells.
I cannot see my valley now.
I crave for lassi
but they bring us rusty water
in the bottom of a can.

They come and come,
day, night, day,
unbuttoning
as the door slaps against the stucco.
They leave our thighs and faces
crusty with their stink.

And after me,
they hump across on to my mother,
covering her shrunken face
with her heavy dirndl skirt.
She is dry, dry.
Her womb is a husk.

Each day I am ripening.
I do not want this cuckoo
fluttering its rabid wings
in my darkness.
I can see its wild eyes beneath my skin.
It will suck me dry as rock.

Yet, I have practised its birth –
how I will keep my legs far apart,
my eyes screwed shut,
then roll it with my heel in the dust
kicking it and its afterbirth
down the mountainside.

Or, how I will say, *Give me my baby,*
and boy or girl, call it Katya.
That was my mother's name.

Pat Borthwick

One Thousand Birds
for Sadako Sasaki

In October, up to sixty thousand cranes
pass overhead, skeins of grey across the sky.
Here an installation of white paper cranes,
continuous rain from metal hooks,
birds dance through air, arc to the floor,
the smallest fade into the distance.

Wide windows throw sheets of light.
Sadako is in bed, aged twelve, folding her birds,
one thousand to ward off leukemia.
She was almost two when the bomb flung her
from the breakfast table. Her family crouched all day
in a boat, in radioactive rain near Hiroshima.

Now she folds paper, this way, that way
to make a crane, folding to create the elongated neck,
the elegant sweep of wings. Sadako folds to make
a thousand birds for protection against her illness.
When she dies in October, her friends complete
the cranes, bury them with her.

Rose Cook

Stonemason

*Outside the École des Hospitalières St Gervais, Paris, a plaque
commemorates 165 Jewish children deported in 1942.*

He takes his slab of quarried stone
measures it, cuts to size,
etches the inscription.
No space for names,
just the numbers: one-six-five.
Crystal fragments spill like tears
around his bench, as tungsten
chips the keening marble,
stuttering hammer-head on steel
echoes through the silence
forcing truth from its rocky bed,
ash-white dust clings to his fingers
as he sands and buffs the fine Carrara
smooth as a lip's caress on infant skin.

Margaret Beston

In Slow Motion

She's slapping across the dust
>>*frame by frame*
and the gutters full of sand
in her camel leather shoes,
scouring the rubble
>>>>>>>>*frame by frame*
>>>>>>>>>>>>for the place
where the dead are playing cards.

But they don't look up, they say
Go home old woman it's late,
it's too late now, Can't you see
the sun's burnt out? Our lava brains
have cooled, we're light as pumice.

It's a dream you're in, go home!
Bake us a tray of sand cakes.
– A pair of bombs – look, three straight shells –
sniper flush, a sniper flush –
Don't think you can bury us,

it's a full house already.
Game's up, and you can't deal us
a different hand. Mother, go home.
We've forgotten you for good.
Frame by frame we've forgotten you for good.

M R Peacocke

Nightmare
for my brother

At night he shudders, sweats and cries
On burning deck on sea of stone.
Sodden sheets between his thighs
Duvet white coral, pillow bone.

On burning deck on sea of stone,
He hears a sea that mimics sighs.
Duvet white coral, pillow bone –
Shrouds of flame smear sombre skies.

He hears a sea that mimics sighs.
Galahad, burning hulk, beds down.
Shrouds of flame smear sombre skies:
Brothers sinking, missing, drowned.

Galahad, burning hulk, beds down,
Sodden sheets between his thighs.
Brothers sinking, missing, drowned –
At night, he shudders, sweats and cries.

Lindy Newns

See note p. 159.

'Their Name Liveth For Evermore'

Death's tidied up in rows and lists.
The scratched are 'Known to God'.
'He is not missing, he is here' –
Else in the awkward squad.

His name's got weightier then him.
He's been peeled off from it.
It didn't do much for him in his life.
That went AWOL. Poor fit.

What is it for some name to 'live'?
It's lifeless. Set in stone.
Its bearer proved too slight for it.
He'd always been 'Unknown'.

Denise Riley

See note p. 159.

Testimonial

Pressed flat inside green leather
the stained, worn piece of paper
which he shows to all his carers.

*He gained operational experience
in the Falklands campaign.*

He was nineteen, sent a letter home
from *The Invincible* asking for suntan lotion.

*He is a polite, reasonable man,
works well without supervision.*

                         Now
they will supervise him, change his sheets,
wipe his bum, put food beside his bed, leave.

*He maintained an outstanding level
of fitness and was a serious contender
in national standard triathlons, which
requires dedication and sacrifice.*

                         Now
they are dedicated to keeping him alive,
however much he longs for death.

*Unfortunately, he has decided to
leave the corps before realising
his full potential.*

                         Now,
he is slowly leaving life behind,
without fully realising

*his pleasant, amiable approach
will be missed.*

Lindy Newns

See note p. 159.

138

How It Is
i.m. Sam Alexander, MC

Trestles slide away, folded
and put aside, candles snuffed
the singing stops, the music
dies, mourners drift off
and regroup by the gate

Dear God, there seems
so little now to show for it all
nothing but a rolled-up flag
a scatter of wreaths, a bugle call
this shock of fresh-dug earth

Angela Kirby

between the lines

Archive

They left their mark on pages, stones,
between Usk and Wye, Ebbw, Monnow, bones
in the turned earth of a field, in pit and street,
list and litany, letter, will, receipt,
the etcetera of terraces, a statued square,
all that was left behind of who they were.

Ysgrifen yr afonydd, sibrwd Sirhywi,
Rhymni, Wysg, Gwy ac Ebwy,
geiriau o gariad, stôr o straeon,
gwaith glô, gwaith haearn,
gwaith tir mewn gwynt a glaw,
deilen a dalen yn yr adeilad hwn. *

Read these walls, these pages, history
between the lines of what's most ordinary.

Gillian Clarke

* Scribble of rivers, whisper of Sirhowy,
  Rhymney, Usk, Wye and Ebbw,
  words of love, a store of stories,
  coal-work, iron-work,
  land-work in wind and rain,
  on leaf and page in this house.

No One Said a Word

Off Howdiemont, the sea grows pale.
The sky turns silver-pink. The pools

Brim with light. The oystercatcher
Yelps, the turnstones rise, and over

The North Bay, the red sun flares.
It floods the holes, the Iron Skeers,
The bents, the Bathing House, the wares,

Without a sound. At the Weir Buses,
At Hip's Heugh on the Hinds' Hooses,

Not a single boat. No yellow figure
Squints, beatified, his fingers

Coiling the wet tow, lacing the creeves.
No wake of white gulls ploughs the sea.

No boot-sole print the soft mud track
To Sugar Sands; and down the rocks

No woman bends her shadowy
Four-footed shape at Shallowarry.

The seas break on the Big Skeer,
Slowly roll over, a distant roar,

A taste of iron. A knotted hawser
Twists, a frozen current of water.

Split like an oak-stump, ten feet tall,
Riveted with barnacles,

The great pipe-organ boiler towers.
The seas around it blossom, flower,

Over and over. No one mourns
The countless quiet men and women

Who softly shuffled from this shore,
Their limpet creels, their swulls, their gear,

Their heavy hearts. No, no one heard
Them leave. Nobody said a word.

Katrina Porteous

See note p. 160.

To an Unknown Grandmother

Your picture tells us we don't have your looks -
your black hair, thick as brambles,
low brow, calm gaze, cream skin.

We're not like you

We don't know much: thin glimpses
through a twitched net curtain
dropped as fast as raised.

You sewed fine linen.
Embroidered
wild flowers tamed
in Celtic cubes.
You came from Ireland
worked in the Lake District
met my grandfather
rode south in his sidecar
had two sons
and took three days to die
of Spanish flu.

Was it from Cork or Sligo that you came?
Why did you leave? Who was your family?
No-one was telling.

We're not like you.

Firm in our setting, we belong;
though like an ore seam glinting in dull rock
your Irish eyes flash
through our occasional souls.

Joy Howard

My Cousin

Edith Hemp, d. 1930

She came here – not to rest – to sweep the stairs
and empty chamber pots. The gilded chairs
still stand here; the enormous mirrors throw
my face back as they did hers, aeons ago.
Down the plush corridors she moved, her feet
not echoing – dusting, leaving all things neat.
Somewhere her midget room, a great way up
those stairs. Invisible beneath her cap
to Bournemouth's guests, but I know who she was,
my flesh, my blood, thrust early from the nest.
A small, skimped woman when she was alive,
all siblings lost, unmatched at forty-five.
No trace, not one. Still stands the Grand Hotel,
but now she rests. Somewhere in Bournemouth still.

Merryn Williams

Arbroath

I look among the people on the half-forgotten platform

for him –

Captain Sem,

a while now gone.

Henryk, as my mother's cousin called him,

as we all came to.

Gillian Allnutt

The Carpenter

... and they carried his body
down to *Victory's* belly,
laid him on the hearth
before the galley fire.

Women tried to revive him,
chafe his hands to warmth,
put brandy to his lips.
The man they cradled

had tried to right the ship,
twice cried a warning
to the watch and been ignored
before the waters came.

Dismissed, he drowned as
the *Royal George* went down;
floating with hen-coops
hammocks and splintered masts.

No plaque marks where he lay;
no one speaks his name.

Denise Bennett

The Serving Girl

Though I never knew her
I bear her name.
Margareta. My grandmother.
She is undismissable.
Sitting at the sea's edge
A moon-faced dog at her side.
Eyes – neat as jet.
Skin the colour of turtledoves.
The lick of salt in her hair
Dark with time.

Here, next to her, is a blue pot that mutters.
Let us call it, the sea.
It contains all the words we never spoke.
It is held in our four hands
That never touched.
Fierce as flint, the years that lie between us.
Plaiting and unplaiting the dark memory
Of your hair.
Though I never knew you, I bear your name.

I imagine the stairs you climbed in the grand house.
The starched minute hand of the clock
Ticking in the hall.
The mistress of the house checking your apron.
Your presence in your own absence.
Nothing to be done but bear it.
I imagine the meals on silver trays carried back and forth.
The perfectly folded white cloths.
All with initials. None of them yours.
I can almost smell the blooms of white clematis
As it hung near your window.
In winter they will cut it back, and you will miss it so.

Did the house have a hundred rooms? I want to ask.
And was yours the finest Margareta?
Your secret name that lies on cloth invisible,
That now must serve for memory.
Only her voice, that is the salt, that is the sea,
Answers me.

I swill her voice around my empty head.
I watch the tide that cannot call her home.
A prism of water in my throat. My throat that
glinting, swells, becomes the sea.
A final call that earths two names. A shaft of sunlight.
Our meeting now – like this. Incredible.
The pure chance of her wave ending
Right where mine began.

Helen Burke

Stroyka 501

This is the place, says Lyudmila. *Start digging.*
They hit something metallic and begin scraping.

Rusty nails, a piece of track on the outskirts
of Salekhard, the capital of the Yamal Nenets

Autonomous Region. Once, a 10,000 year old
baby woolly mammoth was discovered buried

near here. It's in a museum now. An attraction.
But this is different. Construction Project 501.

The Great Plan for the Transformation of Nature.
A trans-Polar line stretching from Inta to Igarka,

its workforce, enemies of the people – poets,
a 16 year old orphan caught stealing beetroots

to feed her sisters, soldiers who'd been released
from prisoner-of-war camps, a fresh-faced

book-keeper whose employer's money was eaten
by rats that got in the safe. 300,000 not forgotten,

but not talked about either. A third of them dead
from execution, exhaustion or hunger. The cold

would have taken many more. 50 below in winter.
The project stopped when Stalin died. The tundra

took their bones with the tracks, kept the secret
for half a century. Lyudmila and others collect

statements, photos and letters for the archives,
for the descendants of prisoners and guards who live

side by side now, for future generations, for tourists
who arrive by helicopter. Rumour has it the quest

for gas will resurrect the Great Plan. Outside the gate
of Camp 48, a tourist unzips his padded jacket,

drinks vodka, then tips the remainder in the snow.
He leaves a potato and a loaf of bread before he goes.

Pat Winslow

Lost Boy

Not long after your picture had been filed
the press began to circulate another.
Your brief appearance as 'drowned Syrian child'
was superseded by your little brother.

The media reviewed the human damage
and Don McCullin with his Magnum eye
explained why Aylan's was the single image
your tragedy will be remembered by.

You were too clearly dead; he seemed asleep
He was the Twitter '*Ooh*', the Facebook '*Aww*'.
His was the picture that they chose to keep;
an easy icon for a distant war.

Your likeness now is difficult to find.
Not quite so cute, and yet a lot more true,
uncomfortable, best put out of mind.
This poem, Ghalib Kurdi, is for you.

Ann Drysdale

Freeze 1947

Long ago in the first white world, school closed.
The park disappeared, the lake froze,
the town lost its way, sea struck dumb
on the beach. Birds held their tongues.

Land lay spellbound. World was an ice garden
beyond fern-frozen glass. Trees held out white arms,
waltzed with the wind and froze to stone.
On doorsteps bottled milk stood stunned.

The polar bear rug on the living room floor
rose from the dead, shook snow from its fur
and stood magnificent on all fours,
transfigured, breathing flowers.

And a girl on the road from school was stolen, her breath
a frozen rose, her marble sleep, death.
They hid the paper. 'Babe in the Wood' it said.
I thought of her school desk, its name-carved lid

slammed on slurred air, her face blurred
over books her eyes of ice would never read,
her china inkwell emptied of its words,
the groove for her pen like a shallow grave.

Gillian Clarke

Roses of Picardy

We speed past fields
as rows of poplars disappear across a land
at peace; no men running, falling helpless
in the mud, no crater scars, no screams.
But the earth has a memory

and a voice. I see my father
sunk in a green armchair singing
to himself the words he knew by heart,
his Irish tenor meant for pals
who never grow old.

Geraldine Paine

Kinship

Your house of bones is long lost from our lives.
We think of you as once you lived for us
for you are here inside us at the heart
of all we do. You have no power now
but you are in our genes, our blood, our words,
our thoughts, our past. You still are part of us
for bloodlines move us on in different ways.
Though we forget your face, the things you said,
your family likeness looks out through our eyes.
We carry ancestors around with us:
the boy who never smiled, the aunt who sang.
Our people crumble into air and fade,
long-gone, yet not gone fully from our lives.

Jenny Morris

Postlude

Providence

I have not stumbled down a street in Haiti
with only half the skin on my back.
I have not been taken out of school
and taught to use an AK47 on my family.

I have not spent my adulthood locked up
for a crime I did not do.
I have not been given HIV
from a contaminated blood transfusion.

I have not eked my three-year life out
eating wallpaper. I have not handled methadone
or strapped on explosives.

I have not got God. But I have got to fifty-three
and walked through Chapeltown
and known, and sometimes known.

Julia Deakin

Notes:

p. 52 *A C Clarke* Casualty

Editor's note:

This poem has been translated in to Scots (Sheila Templeton) and Gaelic (Maggie Rabatski) see p. 161.

pp. 74, 102 *Fiona Durance* Nervosa and Clare

Author's note:

These poems do not portray specific individuals but are based on conversations with people who have experienced eating disorders mno have worked in the sex trade. I was strongly encouraged to tell these stories, with some commenting to the effect that no-one would listen to them, but that people might listen to a poet.

pp. 136, 138 *Lindy Newns*

Author's note:

My brother David was a Royal Marine.

'Nightmare' is based on his experiences in the Falklands, where he was one of the youngest marines to serve. He is one of many ex-soldiers dealing with the scars of PTSD.

'Testimonial' A former tri-athlete, David is now suffering from MS. One of the few things he has always kept safe is a green leather wallet containing the testimonial he was given when he left the service. The poem includes extracts from this testimonial.

p. 137 *Denise Riley* 'Their Name Liveth For Evermore'

Author's note:

'Their Name Liveth For Evermore' (From the sequence 'A gramophone on the subject' – part of a commission by The Poetry Society *The Pity* 2014)

This wording appeared on many war memorials. How to name and record the dead of 1914-1918 was a strikingly prominent question. The ideal of dignifying those lost beyond any hope of burial produced the emblematic figure of the Unknown Soldier, 'Their Name Liveth For Evermore' was engraved on many war memorials including the Menin Gate at Ypres. This monument invoked another, would-be consoling rubric; 'He is not missing; he is here'. My speakers offer their own laconic thoughts on this matter of names without bodies, bodies without names.

p. 144 **Katrina Porteous** No One Said a Word

The poem describes the activities of fishermen and their womenfolk near Howick on the Northumberland coast in the early 20th century.

Bents; marram grass. *Buses;* seaweed-covered rocks. *Creeves;* crab and lobster pots. *Hawser;* cable. *Heugh;* a rocky outcrop on land; *Hip's Heugh on the Hinds' Hooses* was a fishing mark at sea. *Hinds;* farm labourers. *Howdiemont;* name of beach near Howick. *Limpet creels;* baskets in which women carried bait on their backs. *Pipe-organ boiler;* remains of wreck of French trawler Tadorne (1913) at Howick. *Shallowarry;* name of rock near Howick where women gathered limpets as bait for long-lines. *Skeers;* outlying rocks. *Swulls;* shallow baskets used to carry long-lines. *Tow;* rope. *Wares;* seaweed.

Addendum

Translations of A C Clarke's 'Casualty'
p. 52

Missthriven

*An faa are ye, puir fushach by the road-
side
thrown oot lik pan-jotrals by a kitchie-
deem?*

I'm naethin, jyst orrals fae a midden-
tap
ye'd see here ony day

*Fit did ye eest tae be
unner sic a sun that shines wi nae peety
unner sic a sky that kens naethin o
tears?*

I wis a leal han held reddy
a mither's bosie
a bairn's feet rinnin

*Fit took ye tae bide in this killin-hoose
sae lang efter the sodgers cam?*

This is ma hame grun
the grun o ma faither's faither
I spik for this place

*Lat me murn the loss o yer licht
mynd aathin that eence wis you?*

Na na. Dinna greet for me.
Saat tears are wersh
will iron-eer bricht howps

Dinna sing murnin psalms
their airels hing ower wechtie

Dinna fesh flooers
their petals splyter

Mak me hale
mak me hale again
vrocht throu wirds
offer up ma name.

Sheila Templeton

Ìobairt

*Cò thu, caithte mar sgudal-taighe
ris a' chabhsair?*

Is neoni mi
seach sprùilleach gach uile là

*Dè ma-tà a bh' annad
fon ghrèin chruaidh seo
fon ghrèin seo nach dèan gul?*

Làmh thapaidh a' smèideadh
pòg màthar
casan aotrom pàiste

*Carson a dh'fhuirich thu
sa bhaile chasgraich
nuair a ràinig na saighdearan?*

Seo far am buin mi
seo dachaigh mo shinnsirean
tha cainnt a' bhaile-sa air mo bhilean

*Cionnas a nì mi do chaoidh
do chumail air chuimhne?*

Na toir thugam dìtheanan
silidh iad an cuid bhileag

Seachain na sailm tòrraidh
cho trom, trom air a' chluais

Cuir casg air do dheòir
mus mìll an geurachd
gach ùr-dhòchas shoilleir

Cruthaich as ùr mi
le cumadh daonnda mar a bha
tog an-àird mi led bhriathran
cuir ainm rium

Maggie Rabatski

Ann Alexander worked as an advertising copywriter in London for many years. She has published four collections of poetry, with Peterloo Poets and Ward Wood. Her last collection, *Old Things*, deals with the loss of her husband and her thirty years in Cornwall. She lives in Stratford upon Avon now.

Gillian Allnutt has published eight collections, including *How the Bicycle Shone: New & Selected Poems* (Bloodaxe 2007). A new collection *wake* is due to be published in 2018. She received The Northern Rock Foundation Writer's Award in 2005 and The Queen's Gold Medal for Poetry 2016.

RV Bailey has published 6 poetry collections: *Course Work, Marking Time, From Me To You* (with U A Fanthorpe), *The Losing Game, Credentials*, and *A Scrappy Little Harvest* (2016). With Stevie Krayer she edited *A Speaking Silence: Contemporary Quaker Poetry*, and with June Hall *The Book of Love & Loss*.

Fran Baillie, having retired from lecturing, proceeded to find a creative spark on the M.Litt at Dundee University. She subsequently published a number of poems and a pamphlet, *Mixter-maxter* (Hen Run 2017). She writes in Scots and English and is presently undertaking two pamphlets: about her mother, and about the vagaries of a Catholic education.

Denise Bennett has an MA in Creative Writing and runs poetry workshops in community settings. Her work has been widely published in poetry journals. She has two full-length collections –*Planting the Snow Queen* and *Parachute Silk* (both Oversteps Books) and a pamphlet collection *Water Chits* (Indigo Dreams)

Margaret Beston is the founder of Roundel, the Tonbridge-based Poetry Society stanza.Her work has appeared in magazines including *The Frogmore Papers, Orbis, South, Prole*, and in anthologies – most recently *Fanfare* (Second Light Publications) with her prizewinning poem, *By Heart*. Her collection, *Long Reach River,* was published in 2013.

Pat Borthwick spent much of her upbringing on the canals and waterways of Britain. She now lives on a farm in the Howardian Hills close to the North York Moors. She works as a freelance writer, a Creative Writing tutor and a Poet in Schools.

Sara Boyes has contributed poems to a number of anthologies, including *Soul Feathers* and *A Star in the Heart,* and has two collections, *Kite* and *Wild Flowers* (Stride, 1989 and 1993) and a pamphlet, *Black Flame* (Hearing Eye, 2005). For many years she taught creative writing in the Faculty of Continuing Education at Birkbeck.

Valerie Bridge has taught Languages and Creative Writing, given Adult Education classes. Writing and has been widely published in magazines and anthologies. A love of words has always been her mainstay and her passion. She also concerns herself with green issues.

Carole Bromley lives in York. She has two collections with Smith/ Doorstop, the most recent being *The Stonegate Devil,* which won the 2016 York Culture Award. A collection for children, *Blast Off,* was published in September 2017.

Helen Burke's new collection is *Today the Birds Will Sing* (Valley Press). Previous collections: *Ruby Slippers* and *Here's Looking at You, Kid.* Widely published here and America, she has read in Paris, New York, Chicago and Rome. Nominated for the Pushcart Prize. She hosts a radio show for poetry in Leeds.

Marianne Burton's pamphlet *The Devil's Cut* was a Poetry Book Society Choice. Her collection *She Inserts The Key* (Seren) was shortlisted for the Forward First Collection Prize 2013. Her next collection is due from Seren in 2018.

Maggie Butt is an ex-journalist and TV producer, turned poet. Her fifth poetry collection is *Degrees of Twilight* (The London Magazine 2015). She is a Royal Literary Fund Fellow at the University of Kent and an Associate Professor of creative writing at Middlesex University, London. www.maggiebutt.co.uk

Alison Chisholm is a poetry tutor and adjudicator, and the author of eleven collections. She writes poetry columns for '*Writing Magazine*', and textbooks on the craft of writing poetry.

Gillian Clarke is President of Tŷ Newydd, the Welsh Writers Centre and was National Poet of Wales 2008 – 2016. In 2010 she was awarded the Queen's Gold Medal for Poetry. *Ice*, (Carcanet), was short-listed for the TS Eliot Award 2012. Picador published *Selected Poems* in 2016. Her latest collection, *Zoology,* was published by Carcanet in 2017.

Rose Cook was born in Yorkshire and now lives in South-West England, where she is a well-known poet and performer. She has a pamphlet *Everyday Festival* (HappenStance), and two collections: *Taking Flight* (Oversteps) and *Notes From a Bright Field* (Cultured Llama). Her new collection with Cultured Llama was published in September 2017. www.rosecook.wordpress.com

Julia Deakin is widely published, has won numerous prizes and featured twice on Poetry Please. Her collections *The Half-Mile-High Club* (a Poetry Business competition winner), *Without a Dog* (Graft 2008), and *Eleven Wonders* (Graft 2012), are praised by leading poets; a new collection is imminent.

Rosemary Doman is a retired tutor in creative writing and English, who writes poetry and short stories. She has been published in various anthologies and magazines and had success in writing competitions.

Ann Drysdale has published six poetry collections, as well as memoir, essays and a gonzo guidebook to the City of Newport. She lives in a mining town in South Wales.

Jane Duran was born in Cuba and brought up in the US and Chile. *Breathe Now, Breathe* (Enitharmon Press 1995) won the Forward Prize for Best First Collection. *Silences from the Spanish Civil War* (2002), *Coastal* (2005), *Graceline* (2010) and *American Sampler* (2014) followed, all from Enitharmon. She received a Cholmondeley Award in 2005.

Fiona Durance has worked as a poet coach, dancer, BSL interpreter and equalities trainer. She has worked extensively with minority and marginalised groups. She believes that structural equality can be dismantled, a fair and respectful society is possible – and that every interaction counts. Her poetry has appeared in many publications.

Elsa Fischer is Dutch-born. She has published in the UK, Ireland and North America. Her pamphlet *Palmistry in Karachi* was published in autumn 2017 by Templar Poetry. She is working on a sequence of poems about life in a retirement home.

Kate Foley lives in Amsterdam when not in Suffolk, where she leads workshops and performs. She has seven full collections, and *Electric Psalms: New & Selected Poems* was published by Shoestring Press in 2016.

Katherine Gallagher is Australian-born and London-based. Her sixth and most recent poetry collection is *Acres of Light* (Arc Publications, 2016). It follows *Carnival Edge: New & Selected Poems* (Arc Publications, 2010). 'Gallagher is a poet of the eye, the rainbow, and of all the feeling senses.' (*Penelope Shuttle*).

Mavis Gulliver lives on the Hebridean Isle of Islay. She watches otters and seabirds from a cabin on the shore of her garden. She writes for *Scottish Islands Explorer* magazine and has two collections published by Cinnamon Press – *Slate Voices: Islands of Netherlorn* (2014) and *Waymarks* (2015).

Susanna Harding works as a theatre practitioner and festival director in partnership with The Royal Exchange Manchester and The New Vic Theatre. Published in *The North, The Frogmore Papers, Smiths Knoll, Equinox, Orbis,* and *New Walk.* She is delighted to be making her third appearance in a Grey Hen Press anthology.

Joy Howard founded Grey Hen Press in 2007. This is the twelfth Grey Hen anthology she has edited and published and she has three collections: *Exit Moonshine* (Grey Hen Press 2009), *Refurbishment* (Ward Wood 2011) and *Foraging* (Arachne Press 2017).

Maria Jastrzębska's selected poems, *The Cedars of Walpole Park*, were translated into Polish (Stowarzyszenie Zywych Poetów 2015). She translated Justyna Bargielska's *The Great Plan B* (Smokestack Press 2017) and her new collection *The True Story of Cowboy Hat and Ingénue* appears in 2018 (Liquorice Fish). www.mariajastrzebska.wordpress.com

Mimi Khalvati has published eight collections with Carcanet Press, including *The Meanest Flower*, shortlisted for the TS Eliot Prize and *Child: New and Selected Poems 1991-2011,* a Poetry Book Society Special Commendation. Her most recent book, *The Weather Wheel,* was a PBS Recommendation and Book of the Year in *The Independent.*

Angela Kirby grew up in rural Lancashire but now lives in London. Her poems are widely published, broadcast and many have been translated into Romanian. Her three collections: *Mr. Irresistible, Dirty Work* and *A Scent of Winter,* and *The Days After Always: New and Selected Poems* (2015) are all published by Shoestring Press.

Pauline Kirk is the author of six novels (three written as PJ Quinn), and ten collections of poetry. She is also Editor of Fighting Cock Press. A new poetry collection and a fourth PJ Quinn novel, *Poetic Justice*, are due out in late 2017.

Wendy Klein was born in New York, and left the US in 1964. A retired psychotherapist, she has spent most of her adult life in England. She has two collections from Cinnamon Press: *Cuba in the Blood* (2009), *Anything in Turquoise* (2013) and a third, *Mood Indigo,* from Oversteps Books.

Stevie Krayer's publications include three collections and an anthology, *A Speaking Silence: Quaker Poets of Today* (co-edited with R V Bailey). Her latest collection is *New Monkey* (Indigo Dreams, 2014). She lives in Wales with her husband, writer David N Thomas, a judicious 40 minutes from the grandchildren.

Gill Learner has won a number of prizes, including the Poetry Society's Hamish Canham award, and been published in many magazines and anthologies including previous Grey Hen publications. Her collections, *The Agister's Experiment* (2011) and *Chill Factor* (2016), are from Two Rivers Press. More details can be found at www.poetrypf.

Janet Loverseed is a retired teacher whose poems have twice been prizewinners in the Grey Hen competition. Her first full collection, *The Shadow Shop*, is published by Oversteps Books.

Mandy Macdonald is an Australian writer and musician living in Aberdeen. Her poems appear in two other Grey Hen Press anthologies, *Outlook Variable* and *Extraordinary Forms*, and in numerous other places in print and online, most recently in *The Curlew, Three Drops from a Cauldron*, and *Clear Poetry*.

Fokkina McDonnell recently retired. Dutch-born she has lived in the UK for most of her adult life. Poems have been placed in competitions, and appeared in anthologies and magazines, including *Magma, Orbis, The North, Mslexia, Poetry News.* Oversteps Books published her debut collection *Another life* (2016). Fokkina blogs on www.acaciapublications.co.uk

Rosemary McLeish was born in 1945. She is an artist as well as writing poetry. She moved to Kent six years ago, since when poetry has taken a backseat to art, though it is now raising its head again with several performances. She was recently published in the Medway-based magazine *Confluence*.

Char March's poem won the 'Remember Oluwale' poetry competition. She urges you to find out more about David, and to donate to the *David Oluwale Memorial Association* to help in their excellent work with migrants and people with mental health problems. Her latest poetry collection is *The Thousand Natural Shocks* (Indigo Dreams).

Jenny Morris has taught in this country and abroad. Her poems and fiction have been widely published in collections, anthologies and magazines. Her work has appeared in eight Grey Hen Press anthologies. She lives in Norfolk.

Jane Monach grew up in Belfast, travelled, and now lives in Sheffield, where she writes and explores poetry and prose with a number of groups. She has worked in mental health and education.

Cheryl Moskowitz is a poet, novelist and translator. She writes for children and adults and since 2014 has been Poet-in-Residence at Highfield Primary School in North London. Publications include novel *Wyoming Trail* (Granta, 1998), poetry collection *The Girl is Smiling* (Circle Time Press 2012), poetry for children *Can it Be About Me?* (Frances Lincoln, 2012).

Anne B. Murray worked for many years in Glasgow Adult Learning encouraging individuals and groups to read and write poetry. Now retired and based in Stirling, she writes and performs poetry and continues to facilitate public readings. She has had many poems published in several journals and anthologies.

Frances Nagle's full-length collection *Steeplechase Park* was published by Rockingham Press. Since then she has been reincarnated as a grandmother and is entering her second childhood with her four grandchildren. She flits between Manchester and Stockport and cycling holidays in Europe. She always carries a notebook and pen.

Helena Nelson runs Happen*Stance* Press. Her most recent book of poems (light verse) is *Down With Poetry!* (Happen*Stance*, 2016).

Lindy Newns has come to poetry seriously only recently. She has been commended for the Portico prize, shortlisted for the Hysteria poetry prize and the Wirral Firsts prize, and published in *Orbis*. She also read her work at spoken word events around Manchester, including the 2017 Didsbury Literary Festival.

Grace Nichols was born and educated in Guyana. She has been living in Britain since 1977, and has received many awards and honours. She is among the poets on the current GCSE syllabus and is a fellow of The Royal Society of Literature. Her latest poetry collection is *The Insomnia Poems* (Bloodaxe 2017).

Ruth O'Callaghan has 7 collections of poetry, been translated into six languages, reads in Asia, Europe and U.S.A. A mentor, reviewer, international competition adjudicator, she leads workshops in UK and abroad. The Arts Council awarded her a grant to work in Mongolia, the XXX WCP awarded a gold medal for poetry in Taiwan.

Jennie Osborne lives in South Devon and is active in poetry around the South West, as well as being a counsellor. She has two collections from Oversteps Books, *How to be Naked* and *Colouring Outside the Lines,* and is one of the organisers of the annual Teignmouth Poetry Festival.

Kathy Pimlott's pamphlet *Goose Fair Night* (Emma Press) was published in 2016. Her poems have appeared widely in magazines including *Magma*, *Brittle Star*, *The North* and Poem, in anthologies and on-line. Born in Nottingham, she lives and works in Covent Garden.

Geraldine Paine has been published in many magazines and anthologies. She is an award-winning poet with an M. Phil in Writing (University of S. Wales), and three collections from Lapwing Publications (Belfast): *The Go-Away-Bird* (2008), *The Beginnings of*

Trees (2013), and *Disappearing Tracks* (2016)). She is a founder-member of the poetry group *Scatterlings*.

Meg Peacocke Born 1930. The usual things, and then many years keeping a smallholding on my own. The 'facts' of my life don't feel as important to me as my observations of the natural world and of some people. My poems usually concern those, sometimes as attempted exorcisms.

Jo Peters is a retired teacher and lives in Yorkshire. She has been published in several magazines and anthologies and has had success in a number of competitions. Her pamphlet *Play* is published by Otley Word Feast Press. When she is not writing she is gardening, looking for wild flowers and spending the kids' inheritance.

Patricia Pogson trained as an artist and travelled widely as a young woman. She settled in Cumbria in her early thirties and started writing poetry. Her work, described by Eva Saltzman as 'poetry for grown ups' has been much anthologised and won major prizes.

Katrina Porteous lives on the Northumberland coast and has written extensively about local inshore fishing traditions. Her poetry collections from Bloodaxe Books include *The Lost Music* (1996) and *Two Countries* (2014), which was shortlisted for the Portico Prize 2015.

Sheenagh Pugh lived for many years in Wales but now lives in Shetland. She has published many poetry collections with Seren, also two novels and a book on fan fiction. Her latest collection is *Short Days, Long Shadows* (Seren 2014)

Eveline Pye has an international reputation for mathematical and scientific poetry and is the only poet to be published in *Significance*, the magazine of the Royal Statistical Society . She was mentored by Liz Lochhead under the Clydebuilt scheme. Her collection, *Smoke That Thunders,* was published by Mariscat Press (2015).

Maggie Rabatski comes from the Isle of Harris but lives in Glasgow. Her work has been published in various anthologies and magazines and she has two pamphlets from New Voices Press, *Down From The Dance* and *Holding*. She writes in both Gaelic and English.

Denise Riley wrote *War in the Nursery* (1983); *'Am I that Name?'* (1988); *The Words of Selves* (2000); *The Force of Language*, with Jean-Jacques Lecercle (2004); *Impersonal Passion* (2005) and *Time Lived, Without Its Flow* (2012). Her main poetry collections are *Dry Air* (1985), *Denise Riley: Selected Poems* (2000), and *Say Something Back* (2016).

Jo Roach's poems come from her powerful pasts – Irish ancestors, Catholic faith, London life and loss – transformed into luminous moments of time for the here and now. *Robert Seatter*

Elisabeth Rowe read English at Oxford and worked as teacher, Citizens Advice Bureau Manager and Social Worker. She enjoys writing in both serious and comic modes. Her three collections are *Surface Tension* (Peterloo Poets), *Thin Ice* and *Taking Shape* (Oversteps Books). Married, with three children and (poetry-writing) grandchildren, she lives on Dartmoor.

Kate Rutter has been an actor in TV, Theatre and film for 40 years. Most recently she played Ann in Ken Loach's *I, Daniel Blake*. Her poems have been published in the anthology *Millstone Grit* (Antiphon Press) and in *Magma*, *Matter*, and *The North*. She was shortlisted for The Bridport Prize.

Fiona Sampson, published in thirty-seven languages, has received a number of national and international awards for her writing. A Fellow of the Royal Society of Literature, she has an MBE for services to literature. As well as poetry, she publishes biography, writing about place, and criticism.

Margaret Speak was a primary school and special needs teacher and also taught adult literature and creative writing. She has written reviews for poetry journals, won prizes with both poems and short stories and been widely published in magazines. She was joint founder of The Yorkshire Open Poetry Competition and is coordinator of York Poetry Workshop.

Anne Stewart founded and runs the online poet showcase www.poetrypf.co.uk. She is Administrator for Second Light, a Poetry Society Stanza Rep, and a past-President of the Shortlands Poetry Circle. Her awards include The Bridport Prize, The Southport Prize, Silver Wyvern (Poetry on the Lake, Italy) and a Hawthornden

Fellowship.

Hilary Stobbs lives on the outskirts of Aberdeen and despite being brought up in the South of England she has always enjoyed the pull Northwards to a broad sky and a landscape that is less tamed. She has a particular affinity with the extremity of the Northern Isles and the dialogue between land and water.

Martha Street was born in America but has been a European for nearly forty years. She lives in Bristol and belongs to Bus Pass Poets, who meet in the city's libraries. A member of Second Light network, she has a collection *Stone Soup* (Palores Publications 2010).

Susan Taylor has seven published poetry collections, the latest two being *A Small Wave for your Form* and *Temporal Bones*, published by Oversteps Books. She holds a Masters degree in Creative Writing from Bath Spa University. Her former life as a shepherd feeds her keen interest in the natural world.

Sheila Templeton is a prize winning Scottish poet. Her latest collections are *Owersettin* with Tapsalteerie Press, 2016, a collaborative pamphlet with two other poets and *Gaitherin,* a full collection with Red Squirrel Press, 2016. She has a website at www.//sheilatempletonpoet.com

Susan Utting's fourth poetry collection *Half the Human Race: New & Selected Poems* was published by Two Rivers Press in 2017. It includes poems from three previous collections, alongside new work reflecting and developing earlier themes of the lives of women, particularly those who are too often overlooked, unseen, hidden, or silenced.

Josie Walsh lives in Wakefield, where for ten years she founder-edited *Under Glass,* a community poetry magazine at Pugneys Country Park. Commended in national competitions with work published in magazines and anthologies, she has two full-length collections published, *Breathing Space* (2004) and *Another Breath* (2009); a third book is near completion.

Jean Watkins lives near Reading. Her poems have appeared in many anthologies and magazines. Two Rivers Press published her collection *Scrimshaw* in 2013 and a second collection is forthcoming from them in 2018.

Christine Webb spent her working life in education. Her first collection, *After Babel*, was published by Peterloo Poets in 2004 and her second, *Catching Your Breath* (celebrating and mourning her partner of 40 years) by Cinnamon Press in 2011. Her poems have appeared in a range of anthologies and magazines.

Merryn Williams has published four collections of poetry and edited several anthologies, including *The Georgians 1901–30*, *Poems for Jeremy Corbyn* (Shoestring) and *Strike Up the Band* (an 80th birthday tribute to John Lucas). She was the founding editor of *The Interpreter's House*. She lives in Oxford with her husband.

Pat Winslow has had seven collections published; most recently *Kissing Bones* by Templar Poetry. She works in schools, care homes, hospitals and prisons as well as with refugee groups. Pat is also a Humanist celebrant. For more information see: www.patwinslow.com and https://thepatwinslow.blogspot.co.uk/

Dilys Wood is poet, poetry tutor and the editor (jointly with others) of six anthologies of women's poetry including *Fanfare*, 2015, *Her Wings of Glass*, 2014, *Images of Women*, 2006. In 1994, she founded the Second Light organisation, a network of around 350 published women poets actively supporting each other's poetry.

Liz Woods was born in Yorkshire and her poetry loving father read Tennyson to her as soon as she progressed from nursery rhymes. She has written poetry all her life and is a previous contributor to Grey Hen publications. She is the author of *Cornish Feasts and Festivals*, published in 2013.

Lynne Wycherley lives on a headland in the West Country. She combines poetry with health research and is a contributor to *The Ecologist* (online). Her *Listening to Light: new & selected poems* was published by Shoestring Press in 2014.

Index of Poets

Acknowledgements

FRAN BAILLIE 'The Drunken Chiel Chats ti the Muin' *Mixter-maxter* (Hen Run 2017). DENISE BENNETT 'The Carpenter' *Parachute Silk* (Oversteps Books 2015). MARGARET BESTON 'Stonemason' published in *The French Literary Review*. SARA BOYES 'Neighbour' in *There Are No Strangers* (Word for Word 2015). CAROLE BROMLEY 'Tom Makes his Mark' *The Stonegate Devil* (Smith/Doorstop, 2015). MARIANNE BURTON 'Grace Before Meals' published in *Poetry News*. MAGGIE BUTT 'The Patron Saint of America' *Sancti Clandestini - Undercover Saints* (Ward Wood 2012). ALISON CHISHOLM 'Outside' *A Fraction from Parallel* (Caleta Publishing 2016). A C CLARKE 'Casualty' *In the Margin* (Cinnamon Press 2015). GILLIAN CLARKE 'Archive and 'Freeze 1947' *Ice* (Carcanet 2012). ROSE COOK 'One Thousand Birds' *Notes from a Bright Field* (Cultured Llama 2013). JULIA DEAKIN 'Coast' and 'Providence' *Eleven Wonders* (Graft Poetry 2012) JANE DURAN 'Where Did They Go?' and 'Road to the French Border, 1939' *Silences from the Spanish Civil War* (Enitharmon Press 2002).ELSA FISCHER 'Memory Ward' *Palmistry in Karachi* (Templar Poetry 2017). KATE FOLEY 'Roots' and 'A Short Chapter in the History of Stone' *Electric Psalms* (Shoestring Press 2016). KATHERINE GALLAGHER 'Bullies' *Acres of Light* (Arc Publications 2016). MAVIS GULLIVER 'Christina MacDonald 1881' *Slate Voices: Islands of Netherlorn* (Cinnamon Press 2014). JOY HOWARD 'Collaboratrice' and 'Clearances – South Harris' *Refurbishment* (Ward Wood 2011). MARIA JASTRZĘBSKA 'Magadan' published in *Poetry Review*, 'Are We Vermin, Mama?' in the project*White Other* commissioned by The Free Word Centre. MIMI KHALVATI 'The Blanket' *The Weather Wheel* (Carcanet 2014). ANGELA KIRBY 'Bird Woman' published in *Litmus 1*, 'Immigrant' *Mr Irresistible* (Shoestring Press 2005). 'How It Is' *A Scent of Water* (Shoestring Press 2013). PAULINE KIRK 'Refugees' *Walking to Snailbeach: Selected and New Poems* (Redbeck Press 2004). WENDY KLEIN 'On a Road near Koronovo' *Anything in Turquoise* (Cinnamon Press 2013). STEVIE KRAYER 'Facts on the Ground' *New Monkey* (Indigo Dreams 2014). GILL LEARNER 'Chill Factor' *Chill Factor* (Two Rivers Press 2016). CHAR MARCH 'Son of the Mother-whose-children-are-like-fish' *Remembering Oluwale* (Valley Press 2016). JENNY MORRIS 'Kinship' *Keeping*

Secrets (Cinnamon Press 2015). LINDY NEWNS 'Nightmare' in *Gazing at Gaia* (Manchester Pots 2017). GRACE NICHOLS 'Two Old Black Men on a Leicester Square Park Bench' *The Fat Black Woman's Poems* (Virago 1984, Little, Brown Book Group). RUTH O'CALLAGHAN 'Miss Hathaway Sweeps Her Path in Autumn 1916' *Vortices* (Shoestring 2016). GERALDINE PAINE 'Roses of Picardy' and 'Morning Men' *The Beginnings of Trees* (Lapwing Publications 2013). MEG PEACOCKE 'Dinka Labourers in Khartoum '*Speaking of the Dead* (Peterloo Poets 2003), 'Her Photo' *In Praise of Aunts* (Peterloo Poets 2008), 'In Slow Motion' *Caliban Dancing* (Shoestring Press 2011). JO PETERS 'The Psalm of Those who Tend the Flocks' *Play* (Otley Word Feast Press 2015). KATHY PIMLOTT 'Apprentice Cutter' *Goose Fair Night* (Emma Press, 2016). PATRICIA POGSON 'Alzheimer's and 'Psychosis' *A Crackle from the Larder* (Redbeck Press 1991, 'Minority' *The Tides in the Basin* (Flambard Press 1994). KATRINA PORTEOUS 'The Blue Lonnen' and 'No-one Said a Word' *Two Countries* (Bloodaxe Books 2014). SHEENAGH PUGH 'The Boy with a Cloud in His Hand', 'Night Nurses in the Morning' and 'Easter' *Later Selected Poems* (Seren 2009). The Winchman on Oscar Charlie' published in *PN Review*. EVELINE PYE 'The Bride' published in *West Coast Magazine. 'Under the Mubaba Tree' Smoke That Thunders (Mariscat Press 2015).* DENISE RILEY 'Their Name Liveth For Evermore' *Say Something Back* (Picador 2016). JO ROACH 'Ghost in the Machine' *Oxford Poets 2007: An Anthology.* 'Place' *Dancing at the Crossroads* (Hearing Eye 1997). FIONA SAMPSON 'Song of the Stepchild' *Coleshill* (Chatto & Windus 2013). MARGARET SPEAK *The Firefly Cage* (Redbeck Press 1998). ANNE STEWART 'Tonight I met Someone' in *Only Here Till Friday* (Bibliotecha Universalis, Aula Magna Series Eng/ Rom 2015; Eng/Sp 2016). HILARY STOBBS 'Woman Through Binoculars' *Until It Rains* (Hen Run 2016). MARTHA STREET 'My Shirt' in *Fanfare* (Second Light Publications 2015). SUSAN TAYLOR 'Cultivators' *Lincoln Green* (Lincolnshire & Humberside Arts 1977). SHEILA TEMPLETON 'Dislocation' *Gaitherin* (Red Squirrel Press 2016). SUSAN UTTING 'The Florist's Assisstant' and 'The Hush-Hush Girl'*Half the Human Race:New & Selected Poems* (Two Rivers Press 2017). JEAN WATKINS 'Our Dream' in *Reading Creative Arts Anthology* 2017. CHRISTINE WEBB 'Cocklers' *Catching Your Breath* (Cinnamon Press 2011). MERRYN WILLIAMS 'My Cousin' *Letter to My Rival* (Shoestring Press 2015).

Joy Howard is the founder of Grey Hen Press, which specialises in publishing the work of older women poets. Her poems have featured in many anthologies and journals and can be found online at *poetry p f.* She has edited eleven previous Grey Hen Press anthologies, and published a collection of her own poems *Exit Moonshine* about her 'coming out' experiences in the 1980s. Her second collection, *Refurbishment*, was published by Ward Wood in 2011, and her most recent, *Foraging*, by Arachne Press in 2016.